FEAST YOUR EYES

FEAST YOUR EYES

The Unexpected Beauty of Vegetable Gardens

SUSAN J. PENNINGTON

UNIVERSITY OF CALIFORNIA PRESS   BERKELEY   LOS ANGELES   LONDON

IN ASSOCIATION WITH SMITHSONIAN INSTITUTION TRAVELING EXHIBITION SERVICE   WASHINGTON, D.C.

Published on the occasion of an exhibition from the
Smithsonian Institution, Horticulture Services Division,
and organized for travel by the Smithsonian Institution
Traveling Exhibition Service.

Smithsonian Institution

University of California Press
Berkeley and Los Angeles, California
University of California Press, Ltd.
London, England

Edited by Ann C. Easterling
Text © 2002 Susan J. Pennington

Library of Congress Cataloging-in-Publication Data
Pennington, Susan.
    Feast your eyes : the unexpected beauty of vegetable
gardens / Susan J. Pennington.
        p. cm.
    Includes bibliographical references (p.)
    ISBN 0-520-23521-5 (cloth : alk. paper) — ISBN 0-520-
23522-3 (paper : alk. paper)
    1. Vegetable gardening—History. 2. Vegetables—
History. 3. Gardens—History. 4. Gardens—Design—
History. I. Smithsonian Institution. Traveling Exhibition
Service. II.
    Title.

SB320.5 .P45 2002
635.09—dc21   2002025906

Manufactured in Canada
10 09 08 07 06 05 04 03 02
10 9 8 7 6 5 4 3 2 1

The paper used in this publication meets the minimum
requirements of ANSI/NISO Z39.48-1992(R 1997)
(*Permanence of Paper*). ∞

Frontispiece
The nine square beds or parterres of the sixteenth-century
Château Villandry are the estate's vegetable gardens,
covering 12,500 square meters (134,500 square feet) and
blossoming with thousands of plants. While this particular
garden dates to the early twentieth century, the owner of
this Loire Valley château turned to seventeenth-century
designs to re-create ornamental vegetable gardens in
which careful attention is paid to both beauty and function.
Photo: Charles C. Benton

For Lewis, who left, Anna, who arrived, and Diane Wallace, wherever she is

CONTENTS

ACKNOWLEDGMENTS   I would like to thank Elizabeth Goldson and Ann C. Easterling, my editors at the Smithsonian Institution Traveling Exhibition Service. Liz first broached the idea of doing a book and was a steadfast supporter. Ann Easterling, who should have her name on the cover with me, could not have been kinder, more supportive, perceptive, or patient. Another invaluable contributor was Joyce Connolly of the Archives of American Gardens (AAG). Her attention to detail resulted in the inclusion of many of the wonderful images in this book. Paula Healy was also an invaluable guide to the collections. However, there would be no AAG without the garden owners and the researchers of the Garden Club of America. Thank you to the former for sharing your gardens and the latter for working so hard to provide a wonderful record for posterity.

I am grateful to Marca Woodhams and Valerie Wheat of the Horticulture Branch, Smithsonian Institution Libraries. Nancy Bechtol of the Horticulture Services Division (HSD) invited me to participate in the American Garden Legacy exhibition series. A very warm thank you to all the HSD staff, especially Walter Howell, Jeff Nagle, Michael Riordan, John Walters, and especially Janet Draper, who went above and beyond the call of duty. And there are all the wonderful people who took phone calls out of the blue: Drs. Jan Stuart, John Dardess, Christine Hastorf, David Freidel, Tad Beaker, and Richard Benjamin. Sondra Freckelton helped me to formulate my ideas about still-life paintings. Lou Barndollar and the Coffeyville Historical Society and Susan Steckman and Richard Shaw at the Paca House in Annapolis, Maryland, granted special access to their properties. I would also like to thank everyone involved in Seattle and at the University of California Press for producing such a beautiful, readable book.

Finally, I would like to thank my family: the aunts, uncles, cousins, and grandma who told me all about their vegetable gardens; a fantastic sister and brother-in-law, who cheered the completion of every page and snapped photos of ornamental kale at gas stations; and my stupendous parents. Mom and Dad, this book is simply the latest hurdle that you have helped me over. You hunted down poems, read drafts, copied images, and never let me lose faith. From the bottom of my heart, I thank you for everything and for giving me the by-words for this project: "Hang on, kid, you are getting to the short rows." While all these people contributed much that is right in this book, anything that is wrong remains my responsibility.

Perhaps I should have entitled this book *Ornamental Vegetables: A Budding Cinderella Story*. Ignoring for the moment that it sounds like a headline crafted by a bad sportswriter, I have come to think of the vegetable garden as the Cinderella of the horticultural world—kept around only for the work that she does, her finer attributes outshone by her flashier floral stepsisters. Over the years, as my dissertation research evolved into a cultural history of vegetable gardens, I have been continually disappointed at the short shrift that vegetable gardens have received from scientists and historians. When I took up my fellowship at the Smithsonian Institution with the intention of expanding my background in garden history, I was not surprised to find that garden historians also provided only a cursory examination of the vegetable garden. Either it rated a brief aside somewhere between the Garden of Eden and the St. Gall Plan or it was treated simply as the earliest, most primitive form of horticulture. For the most part, garden historians have concentrated on the presumably more sophisticated and aesthetically pleasing flower and ornamental gardens. Garden historians work from good authority. European and American garden literature of the eighteenth and nineteenth centuries and most of the twentieth century is replete with references to ugly vegetable gardens, and how they must be hidden from view so as not to mar the grace and delicacy of the formal ornamental garden. Vegetable gardens might have been utilitarian, even necessary, but they were also mundane, if not a bit crude.

In recent years, though, Cinderella has finally made it to the ball. The late 1990s saw a rash of books devoted to creating elaborate ornamental vegetable gardens. The authors of these books transformed the garden layout from utilitarian rows to complex designs. Hues and textures were carefully matched, and intricate, complementary planting schemes were devised. While the more elaborate designs might have daunted an avocational gardener, many people were attracted to the shared tenet of these books—vegetable gardens can be as beautiful as any flowerbed. Because a postmodern, frenetic lifestyle does not offer gardeners the time or space for a half-acre vegetable plot in an expansive backyard, most gardens now perform double duty, providing food and beauty. Vegetables grow in flowerpots and hanging baskets on patios and balconies or in small urban allotments. Everywhere flowers and vegetables now nestle beside each other in companionable harmony.

As I browsed through these ornamental vegetable garden books, I was intrigued by a common source of inspiration that many of them shared: the restored vegetable gardens of Château Villandry in the Loire Valley of France. Inspired by seventeenth-century designs, these beautiful vegetable garden parterres excited much interest. They provided one of the first living glimpses of how vegetable gardens were formerly perceived as complementary to the formal ornamental garden, not alienated from it. Following the example of Villandry, modern authors have found myriad ways to elaborate the vegetable garden. Having an antiquarian turn of mind, I wondered what had happened between these two end points.

LOOKING FOR BEAUTY IN UNEXPECTED PLACES

As luck would have it, I was offered the opportunity to curate an exhibit to explore these ideas. In conjunction with the Smithsonian Institution Traveling Exhibition Service, the Horticulture Services Division of the Smithsonian Institution is producing a series of exhibitions, entitled *American Garden Legacy*, which highlights material from the Archives of American Gardens (AAG). In 1992, the Garden Club of America (GCA) donated its extensive slide library to the Smithsonian Institution. These images, dating from the early twentieth century to recent times, form the core of the AAG. While the oldest material in the collection focuses on the formal gardens of large private estates, GCA members continue to document contemporary gardens, including many more vegetable gardens over the last few years. The AAG, therefore, provided one way to document the changing perception of the ornamental appeal of the vegetable garden.

While material from the AAG formed the basis of the exhibit, images from other Smithsonian collections as well as from other museums around the world helped to document the path between the seventeenth- and the twenty-first-century ornamental vegetable garden. However, that is only part of the story.

As I slowly made my way through the collection of tomes in the Smithsonian's Horticulture Library, I would take an occasional break and wander through the Smithsonian gardens. I would often stop and chat with the staff in charge of the gardens. I remember one conversation that went something like this:

Me (pointing at some bright yellow-green foliage rampaging across the garden): Wow, that's impressive. What is it?

Knowledgeable Smithsonian Horticulture Expert: That's a sweetpotato vine called Margarita.

Me (with an incredulous look): No way. Sweetpotato? Like the sweetpotato you eat? Ipomoea?

KSHE: Yup, same plant. There's also Blackie, dark purple, hard to miss. Really great possibilities. You should see it in a container.

Me (with another incredulous look): Sweetpotato? The one you eat?

I won't subject you to the entire conversation, but it went on like that for quite some time. Such was my introduction to the phenomenon of ornamental vegetables. From that point, I eventually learned about ornamental eggplant, kale, and peppers. The first time I saw ornamental cabbage I was simply thunderstruck. That pink, lacy plant was not my grandmother's cabbage. I became intrigued by the idea that vegetables could stand on their own aesthetic merits within the flower garden. I knew something about the ethnobotany of many of these plants, but this project became an excuse to prance across that fuzzy line between food (read: functional) and flowers (read: frivolous).

As dedicated plant fanatics know, if you look hard enough, you can find that somebody, somewhere, sometime has eaten just about every plant on the planet. Therefore, I decided to concentrate on those species traditionally classed as vegetables whose ornamental appeal comes from the living plant. As a result, I don't have anything to say about corn, even though it is considered a vegetable in modern America. For Native Americans, corn was a staple and of great cultural importance. The modern ornamental, multicolored ears of corn are usually used in arrangements after harvesting; the interest is not really in the living plant. Not to mention, there are many books on the cultural history of corn that deal with its history, uses, and varieties much better than I could.

This book is about two complementary and somewhat related phenomena. On one hand, it is the exploration of the aesthetics or the visual appeal of the vegetable garden. How did vegetable gardens go from being elaborately ornamental in the seventeenth century, to being seen as ugly for centuries after that, to being considered worthy of ornamentation again? This book is not about beauty, which, as always, remains firmly in the eye of the beholder. No one who has sweated in a vegetable garden—however arranged and regardless of what is grown—and seen it come to fruition could ever think it was anything but beautiful. What this book is really about is how the evolution in the aesthetic of formal gardens has changed the perception of the vegetable garden. My simple premise is that if the vegetable garden looked like the formal garden, it was admired. If it did not, it was scorned.

On the other hand, this book is also about the aesthetics of vegetables. I examine how some vegetables started their lives as ornamentals, how others have become ornamentals, and how still others float back and forth across the line. I do this by presenting brief biographies of some of these on-again, off-again ornamental vegetables and by looking at how artists have thought about vegetables throughout history. Neither treatment is exhaustive, but I hope to cast light on how some vegetables have caught horticultural and artistic fancies.

I should also explain what this book is not. I am not a horticulturist; I am an archaeologist and therefore more accustomed to dealing with plants that have been dead for thousands of years. My own gardening skills are nonexistent, and I wreak havoc whenever I venture forth into the living botanical world. But I do love the history of these plants and the humble vegetable garden, and that is what I want to share in this book. I have had the benefit of wise tutelage from my parents and other relatives, all of whom are blessed with green thumbs. I have also benefited from many conversations with the horticulturists and gardeners at the Smithsonian Institution in discovering new and unusual ways that people approach the use of vegetables as ornamentals. However, if one wants to know how to actually grow any of the plants mentioned in this book, your local bookstore is replete with practical gardening guides. I simply seek to place these recent horticultural developments in historical and cultural perspective. In other words, I haven't written a "how-to" book. I've written a "how-come" book.

There is so much more I would have liked to include in this book. Mughal gardens, African gardens, Japanese gardens, Caribbean gardens, and Native American gardens are all beautiful in their own right. Moreover, hundreds of vegetables from around the world have ornamental possibilities and fascinating histories. Perhaps I can visit these traditions and vegetables in the future and give them the attention that they deserve. Consider this book only the first approximation of a topic—vegetable garden aesthetics—not long studied.

Susan J. Pennington

1

OF CABBAGES AND KINGS
Quintinie and the Baroque Vegetable Garden

My advice is to make no parterre; at least I would make none, being persuaded that flowers may be easily dispens'd with; resolving then to employ ones grounds in plants that are for use; that part of the kitchen garden which is most pleasing, ought to be put most within sight of the house.

Jean-Baptiste de la Quintinie, *The Compleat Gard'ner*, 1693

To understand the modern phenomenon of ornamental vegetable gardens, one must travel back in time three hundred fifty years to the court of Louis XIV (1638–1715), the Sun King of France. His palace at Versailles featured a truly magnificent vegetable garden of which Château Villandry is but a pale reflection. Yet the creation of one of history's most beautiful vegetable gardens stemmed from the basest of human emotions—jealousy.

On August 17, 1661, Nicolas Fouquet, finance minister to Louis XIV, invited the king and his courtiers to a fête at his home of Vaux-le-Vicomte. The occasion was a celebration of the recently completed renovation of the house and grounds. By all accounts, the party, which took place primarily in the gardens, was a huge success. Everyone was favorably impressed—everyone, that is, except the king. Louis apparently believed that Fouquet was attempting to outshine the Sun King. Within three weeks of the party, Fouquet was in prison, never to be seen again, and the king had appropriated his architects, his gardeners, and over one hundred of his trees.[1]

Louis put Fouquet's team to work remodeling his hunting lodge at Versailles. Whether from fear

(OPPOSITE) FIG. 1-1
Vaux-le-Vicomte, Melun, France, 1920s–1930s
Smithsonian Institution, Archives of American Gardens, Garden Club of America Collection

(ABOVE) FIG. 1-2
Jean-Baptiste de la Quintinie by William Elder. Frontispiece engraving in *The Compleat Gard'ner*, 1693.

FIG. 1-3
The Palace at Versailles, France, 1920s–1930s
Smithsonian Institution, Archives of American Gardens, Garden Club of America
Collection, photo: Williams, Brown, & Earle, Inc.

of royal displeasure or a sincere joy at the new commission, those men over the next forty years constructed a palace and gardens the likes of which the world had never seen. André Le Nôtre, rightly considered a genius by his contemporaries, designed the grounds. The size was immense. From the west side of the château, the gardens, connected by broad alleys, radiated over a mile. Arrayed along the front of the palace were intricate parterres (see "Parterres"). From these, a long green expanse termed the Royal Alley provided an unobstructed view of the Fountain of Apollo. Another set of fountains lay to the north, and to the south were an orangery and the Lake of the Swiss. Surrounding these were dense plantings of trees carved into geometric sections by smaller alleys terminating at openings filled with more statuary and fountains.

The effect of the gardens at Versailles was overwhelming. Here, nature was organized, controlled, and given order that was centered upon the palace and the king. Orange trees bloomed on command. Flowers marched along borders like disciplined soldiers. Trees were carved into elaborate topiaries. View after view terminated in exploding cascades of fountains and statues of Greek gods. As garden historian Christopher Thacker describes it, "The natural world . . . was not in itself beautiful or admirable, but lacking in beauty, proportion and harmony until man had brought it under control and imposed on it his man-centered order, balance and symmetry."[2]

All that could be said about the formal gardens at Versailles could also apply to the *potager du roi,*

the "king's vegetable garden." Among those appropriated from Fouquet's staff was Jean-Baptiste de la Quintinie (Quintyne), whom King Louis placed in charge of the palace vegetable garden and orchards. Quintinie had been born sometime between 1624 and 1626. After touring Italy as a young man, he had abandoned thoughts of a legal career and had taken up the study of gardening, including practical training in vegetable gardening from professional market gardeners.[3]

Quintinie's first task at Versailles was to relocate and enlarge the small vegetable garden of Louis's father. While the best soil was found at some distance from the palace, Quintinie decided to place the *potager* near the palace, in part because Louis enjoyed visiting the garden. Therefore, the new garden was located behind the Lake of the Swiss. The excavated dirt from the lake became the soil of the *potager*. The new vegetable garden was to be in scale with the rest of the gardens of

Versailles. Its outer walls enclosed nine hectares (approximately twenty-two acres). At the center was a large square garden with sixteen beds arranged around a central fountain. This was the main vegetable garden.

Surrounding the large square were more than twenty smaller gardens. The sculpted forms and colorful fruits of espaliered trees festooned the walls. A terrace surrounded the entire vegetable garden so that onlookers could admire the ripening fruits and vegetables. The multitude of sheltering walls and hotbeds allowed Quintinie to produce food year-round for the king's table. Louis was a gourmand and delighted in the delicacies that Quintinie cultivated. Courtier Madame de Sévigné noted: "The subject of peas continues to endure, the impatience to eat them, the pleasure in having eaten them, and the joy of eating them again are the three points that our princes have discussed for the last four days."[4] Louis often visited the *potager* and

FIG. 1-4
Fountain at Versailles, 1900s–1920s
Smithsonian Institution, Archives of American Gardens, Thomas W. Sears Collection

FIG. 1-5
Versailles parterre, 1920
Smithsonian Institution, Archives of American Gardens, Garden Club of America Collection

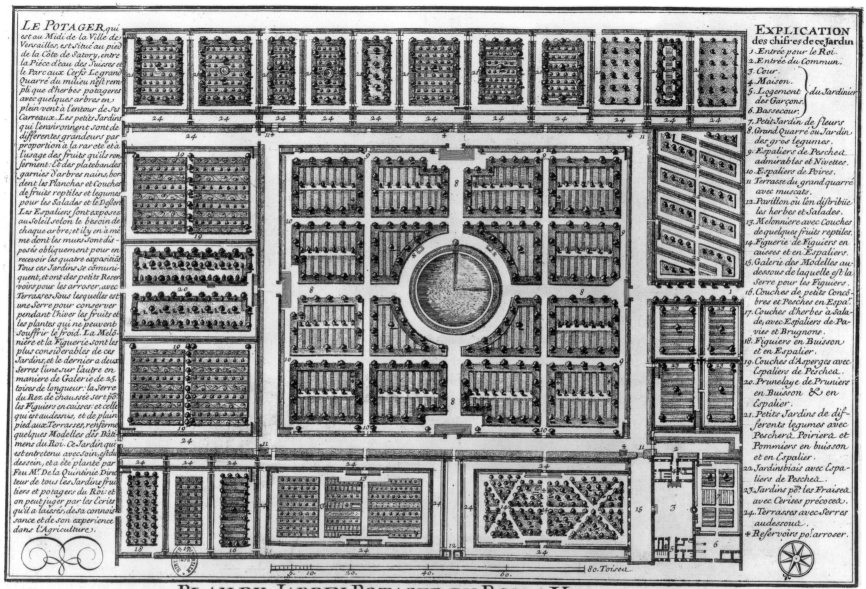

PLAN DU JARDIN POTAGER DU ROY, A VERSAILLES

Fait par Perelle. A Paris chez N. Langlois, rue St Jacques à la Victoire Avec Privil. du Roi

talked with Quintinie, occasionally bringing important visitors like the ambassador of Siam or the
doge of Venice. The king was so pleased with
Quintinie's work that he ennobled him. When
Quintinie died in 1688, Louis remarked that he had
suffered a great loss that would never be replaced.[5]

In 1690, Quintinie's son published his father's
Instruction pour les jardins fruitiers et potagers,
which was translated into English in 1693 under
the title *The Compleat Gard'ner.* In this influential
work, Quintinie gives a clear statement about the
aesthetics of the kitchen garden in the seventeenth
century and the *potager*'s relationship to the formal
garden. In addition to providing instruction on
proper gardening technique, Quintinie wished "to
give such directions, that the place designed for a
kitchen-garden may be so well ordered in all its
parts, [so as] to allure the spectators, and at all
times to delight the eyes of the curious."[6] For
Quintinie, beauty in a *potager* arose from a geometric neatness and an overall balanced symmetry,
an aesthetic sense he shared with Le Nôtre. The
layout of the king's *potager* can actually be seen as
a simplified parterre. Quintinie stated: "The finest
figure that can be desir'd for a fruit or kitchen-garden,

and even the most convenient for culture, is without doubt that which forms a beautiful square."[7]
Even though the plants of the vegetable garden were
not always "pleasing to the eye or smell," Quintinie
recommended forgoing a flowery parterre in favor of
a pretty vegetable garden, if space was limited.[8]

Always a practical man, Quintinie did not
believe in ornamenting the vegetable garden at the
expense of production. He preferred square beds not
only for their regular aesthetic but also for the ease
of working in them: "Whence it is easie to con-
clude, how much I dislike in the case of kitchen-
gardens, all other indented figures, diagonals,
rounds, ovals, triangles &c. which are only proper
for thickets and parterres, or flower gardens, in
which places they are at once both very useful and
of a great beauty."[9] Quintinie also noted that vegetable gardens should be walled in order to protect
the garden from predators and to shelter the plants
from inclement weather, even though the view
from the garden would be sacrificed: "I am not very
desirous of those open prospects which are so necessary for other gardens; . . . a kitchen garden might
have the finest prospect in the world, and yet
appear to me very ugly in itself, if wanting any

FIG. 1-7

Eleutherian Mills, Wilmington, Delaware, 1985

In 1803, Eleuthere Irenee duPont constructed a new home for his family outside of Wilmington. Named Eleutherian Mills, the house was located on the crest of a hill overlooking the Brandywine River. DuPont had studied botany in France, and decided to create an ornamental *potager* for his vegetable garden. Laid out in rectangles and edged by neat gravel paths, the beds were filled with vegetables and colorful flowers. Rose bushes were scattered throughout the vegetable garden, and fruit trees that were trained into conical shapes bordered the garden. Subsequently restored through historical research and archaeological excavation, duPont's *potager* is a source of historical inspiration for the modern gardener.

Smithsonian Institution, Archives of American Gardens, Garden Club of America Collection, photo: Eleanor C. Weller

FIG. 1-8
William Paca was a wealthy Maryland planter and signer of the
Declaration of Independence. Between 1763 and 1765, he built a large
townhouse in Annapolis. While most of his papers and much of the
original grounds were later destroyed, archaeological excavation and a
painting by Charles Willson Peale have allowed the Historic Annapolis
Foundation to reconstruct not only Paca's pleasure ground but also a
small vegetable garden. While it is unknown what exactly Paca planted in his vegetable garden, horticulturists have arranged fruits and
vegetables in beautiful layouts, allowing the modern visitor to catch
a glimpse of the ornamental vegetable gardens of the seventeenth and
eighteenth centuries.
Courtesy of The Historic Annapolis Foundation

FIG. 1-9

A View of Hampton Court, Leonard Knyff, c. 1703

The most successful adaptation of the French baroque to England was at Hampton Court Palace during the reign of William and Mary (1689–1702). With Hampton Court their main residence, William and Mary commissioned Christopher Wren to build a new palace encompassing the older Tudor structure. At the same time, new gardens were designed by London and Wise. Goose-foot parterres ornamented with statues and fountains radiated from the east of the palace. To the north, the Tudor orchard was transformed into a thick woodland maze. Along the south side of the palace were the privy or private gardens, which in Tudor times supplied vegetables and fish from a series of pond gardens. The large, walled vegetable garden that lay to the west shared many features with Versailles's *potager*.

The Royal Collection ©2001, Her Majesty Queen Elizabeth II

FIG. 1-10

Henry VIII's pond gardens at Hampton Court Palace were transformed into flower gardens during the reign of William and Mary. These pond gardens, combined with the recently restored parterre, demonstrate how easily a vegetable garden could echo the formal garden.

Photo: Ann C. Easterling

Parterres originated in Italy, evolving from Renaissance knot gardens in which designs of the individual sections bear no relationship to each other. In parterres, the borders between the knots dissolve, and designs are unified and develop on multiple axes of symmetry. According to gardening lore, parterres came to France with Catherine de Medici (1519–1589), the Italian queen of King Henri II. It was in France that the parterre reached its peak development as a style of ornamental gardening.

Claude Mollet (c. 1563–1650), the patriarch of a dynasty of French gardeners, is credited with creating a particular French style of parterre. He introduced the use of box hedges (*Boxus* sp.) to lay out the main design. The monochromatic, easily shaped box hedge allowed the design to become paramount and increasingly complex. The box also flattened the design, pressing it close to the earth. These box parterres were known as *parterres de broderie*, or "resembling embroidery or brocade." By the middle of the seventeenth century, arabesques, monograms, and elaborate scrolls were commonly used designs. Around the box, powdered coal, iron filings, gravel, or brick dust provided crisp, colored borders. Within this context, flowers would only blur the clean lines of the design and appear too irregular. However, flowers were not completely excluded from the parterre. In a style known as *parterre à l'anglaise* or "English parterres," box hedges defined individual compartments that were filled with flowers. More generally, flowers could often be found along the borders of parterres. In one year alone, the gardeners of Versailles imported eighteen million tulips for the king's parterres.[1]

In addition to elaborating the styles of parterres, another significant French innovation was to bring the axes of symmetry of the parterres and gardens into alignment with the house. According to the French design philosophy, the parterres should be the first component of the gardens seen from the house and should "possess the ground" before the site. This orientation from the house outward meant, in some cases, that the pattern of the parterre would disappear if not viewed from that direction.[2]

1. Penelope Hobhouse, *Penelope Hobhouse's Gardening through the Ages: An Illustrated History of Plants and Their Influence on Garden-Style from Ancient Egypt to the Present Day* (New York: Simon & Schuster, 1992), 166, 174.

2. Christopher Thacker, *The History of Gardens* (Berkeley: University of California Press, 1992), 147–148.

Above left: *Le parterre du midi* at Versailles
A *parterre à l'anglaise* at the restored gardens of Versailles reveals the precision required to create such intricate patterns.
© Gail Mooney

thing of what it should have, instead of finding it there, I should be necessitated to go without it, or to have recourse to my neighbours, or my purse."[10] Though burdened with these practical necessities, the *potager* shared many of the elements found in the ornamental gardens of Versailles: a central water feature, careful attention to color, and geometric patterns with well-developed axes of symmetry.

This baroque ideal flowed from Versailles and swept over Europe. Elaborate parterres, topiaries, and orangeries appeared at estates throughout the continent and in England. At the grandest palaces, broad, razor-straight avenues radiated from the mansion, linking individual elements into a coherent whole. For one hundred years, Le Nôtre's creations defined the epitome of art in European ornamental gardens.

At the same time, Quintinie's work echoed across Europe. Other authors produced designs for the vegetable garden more elaborate than Quintinie would have approved of, but the only impediments to treating a vegetable garden like a parterre were practical, not aesthetic. Engravings from this period consistently show neat, geometric vegetable gardens close to the main house and the pleasure grounds. Because the vegetable garden was a simplified reflection of the more complex gardens surrounding it, it too could be seen as beautiful. Yet while Europeans were admiring the graceful lines of their kitchen gardens, half a world away the Chinese had lost sight of the beauty of the vegetable garden in a rush to create living landscape paintings.

FIG. 1-11
Ragged Jack kale planted in the vegetable garden at the William Paca House in Annapolis, Maryland.
Courtesy of The Historic Annapolis Foundation

2

GARDENS OF THE SOUL
Ming Vegetable Gardens

*The idled garden has everywhere grown to weeds, and
the wattle gate is open now to the dogs and pigs. The
last bitter oranges were picked after the frost, but a
few vegetables still linger in the rain.*

Hu Zhi, "On Returning Home from the Haizhi si
on an Autumn Day"

The Ming dynasty in China lasted from approximately 1368 to 1644. The relative political and economic stability of those nearly three hundred years allowed families to accumulate wealth across generations. Toward the end of the dynasty, part of that wealth was expended on the construction of increasingly elaborate ornamental gardens where the Ming elite both hosted social gatherings and sought refuge for quiet contemplation. However, in the early years of the Ming dynasty, it was to vegetable gardens that the literati (elite scholars and bureaucrats) retreated from governmental affairs, often recording musings about their humble vegetable patches in poems and essays. While many of these writings remain untranslated, the work of a handful of modern scholars provides Westerners with tantalizing glimpses of these ancient Chinese vegetable gardens.

Ming dynasty vegetable gardens were located near the house, arranged in rectangular plots called *qi*. A wall or a ditch and hedge usually surrounded them. Many of the species that the Chinese grew are familiar to Western gardeners. Radishes, melons, onions, eggplants, gourds, cabbages, beans, and sweetpotatoes were much prized. Less familiar are taro (*Colocasia* sp.), *wujiapi* (*Acanthopanax spinosus* Mig., a type of ginseng), the edible chrysanthemum, water spinach (a relative of sweetpotato), ginger, sugar cane, and barberry.[1] John Dardess has paraphrased the poems of Ming scholar Liu Song (1321–1381); they set a familiar scene:

*As Liu Sung grubbed about his garden one spring day,
his thoughts, more problematically, ran off in several
different directions. He thought of the coming harvest
from his peach trees, now in blossom, and of the melons
that, months hence, would ripen from the seeds he now
held in his hand. He could dream ahead to soft, sweet,
golden yellow vegetables and to pickled, green-as-jade
relish. He had some firm ideas about gardening technique. . . . When you plant melon, you must leave a lot
of room for the vines to spread. . . . Lettuce you ate raw,
but rape-turnip you could pickle. He half thought of
compiling a handbook on vegetables and a text on*

FIG. 2-1
Box with cover, Chinese,
Ming dynasty, 1403–1424
Carved red lacquer over wood,
7.9 x 26.6 cm
This box shows a palace garden
motif common in Ming art.
Note the large, single rock on the
left side that informs viewers they
are looking at an intimate garden
scene.
Freer Gallery of Art, Smithsonian
Institution, Washington, D.C.

farming, but meanwhile he must have planted his seeds too deep, because nothing has germinated. If the weeds have flowered (he sighed as he hoed them up), then why haven't the melons set fruit? . . . Weeding is toilsome and unending. . . . He has planted (edible) chrysanthemums too close to a tree, which has since leafed out, and is now shading the plants, so that they look sickly. He wishes someone would come relieve him of the watering-pot, so that he can go eat. On top of it all, the tax-assessor has come by to register his mulberry and fruit trees.[2]

Despite the travails associated with working in a vegetable garden, early Ming scholars took special pleasure in the work. Hu Zhi (1517–1585) noted that he had a garden "where I yield the hoe, leaving the books behind."[3] Quintinie would have agreed with Wang Zhi (1379–1462), who delighted in the self-sufficiency made possible by the ten *mu* garden around his house:[4]

What pleasure can match this? . . . my grass, trees, flowers, fruits, melons, vegetables, pigs, chickens, ducks, geese, oxen, fish, and turtles all come to maturity in season through the year. There is such rich variety and abundance that my desires are satisfied, and I need depend on nothing from outside. My pleasure is such that I would not change places with an enfeoffed feudal lord.[5]

These horticultural efforts were so successful that some scholars were able to sell the excess produce from their vegetable gardens to their neighbors.[6] As important as the practical concerns of raising food and providing for one's family and retainers was the idea of working in a garden as a spiritual quest.

The early Ming literati cultivated vegetable gardens at their private residences not only to escape bureaucratic drudgery and court intrigues, but also to facilitate a spiritual quest away from worldly distractions. The ancient Chinese philosophy of Daoism attempts to bring human existence into harmony with the natural world. Both the natural order and the quest to understand it were known as Dao, simply translated "the way." Seekers of the Dao contemplated the rhythms, cycles, forces, both contradictory and complementary—the yin and yang—which animate the world. This deceptively simple quest could take a lifetime because the inherent contradiction of Daoism is that the Dao is ultimately unknowable and even unnameable. Working in a vegetable garden afforded innumerable opportunities for contemplations of the Dao. Observing a plant day after day—watching it drink in rain, unroll its leaves, produce flowers—and seeing insects crawling over it not only made one a good gardener, it also made one a good Daoist. Early

FIG. 2-3
Garden Scene: melons, egg-plants, flowers and two weasels (detail)
Chinese, Ming dynasty, 1368–1644
Handscroll, color on paper; 216.5 x 36.1 cm
Freer Gallery of Art, Smithsonian Institution, Washington, D.C.
Gift of Charles Lang Freer

FIG. 2-4
Mountain Hermitage at Wulu, Li Shida (c.1574–after 1621)
Chinese, Ming dynasty, early 17th century
Album leaf, ink and color on gold-flecked paper, 31.8 x 60.9 cm
The Ming dynasty owner of this garden commissioned several paintings
of his retreat. (The architectural details vary from painting to painting.)
The owner evidently took great delight in celebrating the beauty of his garden.
Freer Gallery of Art, Smithsonian Institution, Washington, D.C.

Ming scholars considered vegetable gardening and agricultural activities ennobling pursuits in part because of the spiritual contemplation that they afforded. Simple rustic living, honest labor, pride in being self-sufficient, and an ongoing spiritual quest are all virtues celebrated in early Ming garden writing.

In the early sixteenth century, a change appears in the nature of private gardening. The literati begin to write of being addicted to the creation and enjoyment of gardens, not humble vegetable patches, but symbolic landscapes constructed in miniature around their homes.[7] The primary reason for the shift was an economic one. As family wealth increased, the virtue of self-sufficiency, as evidenced by personally working in a vegetable garden, was no longer deemed as important.[8] Instead, later Ming literati expended huge sums on the creation of pleasure gardens, where they not only sought the Dao in quiet contemplation, but also entertained friends and family in lively gatherings.

The literati sought inspiration for the appearance of their gardens in landscape paintings. As painter Dong Qichang (1555–1635) explained, "Some gentlemen's gardens can be painted, but my paintings can be gardened."[9] These paintings did not seek to represent the physical reality of the landscape, but to reveal its symbolic import. Craggy cliffs dwarf human figures; gnarled trees stand testament to the passage of time. The same philosophy was followed in the creation of gardens. Gardens crystallize the essence of the natural world and portray it in miniature as a harmonious and beautiful whole. Beauty is a crucial feature in these gardens because it encourages serenity and facilitates meditation.

Paintings and gardens were to be experienced in the same way. Paintings were often on silk scrolls several yards long, slowly unfurled to reveal a scenic panorama or a series of scenes. The typical private garden of the period also unfolded as a series of individual vignettes, linked by doorways or wandering paths. Architecture, not plants, was the organizing feature of these gardens. One walked through a doorway over which was inscribed a fragment of poetry in beautiful calligraphy. Beyond the doorway, a bridge spanned a pond brimming with floating water hyacinth. Around another corner was a jumble of rocks, reminiscent of the mountains of the immortals. Here and there, peonies, azaleas, camellias, and flowering plums provided splashes of color. Each scene in these gardens was nature in miniature, abstracted to a quintessential point, so that a single azalea would say as much as an acre of them; a lone, well-placed rock was an entire mountain range.

While the literati were creating these naturalized gardens for pleasure and contemplation, the vegetable garden did not disappear completely. Nor were the old values of frugality and industrious labor completely forgotten. Consider the case of Qi Biaojia (1602–1645), a successful bureaucrat and well-respected scholar who was so devoted to gardens that he visited more than two hundred during his retirement. In 1635, Qi constructed an elaborate ornamental garden for himself. Yet amidst the rocks, water, belvederes, galleries, and chapels, there was also a vegetable garden. Qi wrote in his diary that a special highlight of his garden was a rare variety of sweetpotato imported from abroad.[10]

An agricultural treatise published in 1603 cited with approbation an earlier work that described vegetable gardens as small plots of intermixed economic and ornamental plants. The treatise states specifically: "Plant tree peonies and [herbaceous] peonies in a vegetable garden and they will flourish particularly well. . . . Beside beautiful flowers and trees you must plant things like onions and shallots, for the stimulation of their musky smell."[11] The more typical late Ming attitude about the vegetable garden is encapsulated in the writings of Wen Zhenheng (1585–1645), who noted in his *Treatise on Superfluous Things*:

As for arbors of beans, vegetable patches or the wild herbs of the mountains, they are of course not odious, but they should form a separate area of several qing *[100* mu*]; it is not an elegant thing to have them planted in a courtyard. . . . It is suitable to order the gardeners to plant a lot of them [green vegetables] to provide side dishes, but this must be done without thoughts of commercial profit, which makes you no more than a vegetable peddler.[12]*

How ironic that a century earlier Wen Zhenheng's great-great-grandfather had alluded to the simple joy of being just such a vegetable peddler.[13]

By the end of the Ming dynasty, vegetable gardens were no longer described as idealized gardens of refuge and contemplation. Instead, the literati wrote of their increasingly elaborate living paintings as sanctuaries from the worldliness of court life. While later literati continued to possess vegetable gardens, they did not write of working in them as had their ancestors. Nor did they see the simple beauty in vegetable gardens as their ancestors had. The vegetable garden, no longer a spiritual refuge of honest labor, became utilitarian and, hence, ugly. This fate was shared by vegetable gardens in Europe, but for slightly different reasons.

3

BANISHING THE
VEGETABLE GARDEN
FROM THE LANDSCAPE

*Gardening may be divided into three species—
kitchen-gardening—parterre-gardening—and landskip,
or picturesque-gardening.*

William Shenstone,
Unconnected Thoughts on Gardening, 1764

The exquisite precision of the French baroque garden slowly gave way to a more naturalistic style of gardening. The English were early proponents of this new horticultural style. After a century of admiring and imitating the gardens at Versailles, English garden critics began to believe "that nature, distorted by great labor and expense, had lost its power of pleasing . . . and that every place was now becoming nearly alike."[1] Essayist Alexander Pope (1688–1744) was an early, particularly piquant critic of the French style of gardening. The excessive use of topiary in gardens was his first target. He lampooned it by crafting satirical advertisements, such as "St. George in Box; . . . will be in a Condition to stick the Dragon by next April."[2] Pope also deplored the rigid symmetry of the baroque gardens, noting that grove simply nodded at grove and "on ev'ry side you look, behold the Wall!"[3] Instead of a garden confined and twisted into elaborate arti-

ficial patterns, Pope advocated to "First follow Nature . . . That Art is best which most resembles her."[4]

The English deconstruction of the baroque garden began simply. Instead of walls, they used sunken ditches, called "ha-ha's," to keep livestock out without obstructing the view. Paths were curved as opposed to arrow-straight. Unlike the grand theaters of the European palaces, intimate scenes were framed around statuary and grottoes. Placid lakes and streams were preferred to the jetting waterworks of Versailles. Gardens were also allowed to develop their own sense of place without having to be specifically related to the axis of the house. At Twickenham, his home in London, Pope implemented many of these new ideas in his garden. While the grounds feature many formal elements, they are connected by a winding path that takes the visitor to individual tableaux. Although his garden's grotto was very popular among visitors, the best known formal element was an obelisk memorial to his mother. Over time, the English rejected all geometry and straight lines, seeking to free nature from the corseted stays of the French garden.

Landscape paintings set the scene, as it were, for these new gardens. As William Shenstone (1714–1763),

FIG. 3-1
Painshill Park, near Cobham in Surrey, England, was the creation of Charles Hamilton, who lived there from 1738 to 1772. The gardens are best known for their combination of classical and picturesque imagery. A well-proportioned temple of Bacchus brings to mind Arcadia, but Hamilton constructed a ruined abbey and a mysterious grotto by a placid lake to provide a more haunting milieu. His large plantation of conifers added a note of "savage beauty" to his gardens. Smithsonian Institution, Archives of American Gardens, Garden Club of America Collection, photo: Edward Van Altena, 1920s–1930s

FIG. 3-2

Located just outside London, Chiswick House was built by Richard Boyle (1695–1753), the third Earl of Burlington, who corresponded with Alexander Pope as to the design of his gardens. The grounds surrounding Boyle's Palladian villa show the early steps in the development of the English landscape style. Formal alleys radiated from the house and led to a serpentine canal with a rustic bridge and cascade, Gothic ruins, and even an occasional sphinx. The small lake, temple, and obelisk form a carefully crafted scene that came into view as visitors wandered the gardens.

Smithsonian Institution, Archives of American Gardens, Garden Club of America Collection, photo: Edward Van Altena, 1920s–1930s

the poet and garden fancier, put it: "Landskip should contain variety enough to form a picture upon canvas; and this is no bad test, as I think the landskip painter is the gardiner's best designer."[5] Eventually, landscape painting gave its name to landscape gardening from which we derive the modern term "landscaping." The goal of landscape designers, or place makers, as some preferred to call themselves, was to facilitate the experiencing of nature. However, this was not nature, wild and untamed, but romanticized and viewed through the lens of classical allusion. Greek and Roman temples often adorned these nature gardens. Nevertheless, free-flowing landscapes with expansive vistas represented the ideal for gardens from the middle of the eighteenth century onward. There is one difficulty, though, in creating huge parklands, dotted with grottoes, large lakes, extensive lawns, and temples. The area given over to the landscape garden could not easily be combined with land used for food production, whether fields or vegetable gardens.[6]

Initially, some gardening authors did attempt to keep the vegetable garden in the new landscapes. In 1742, Stephen Switzer (1682–1745), an early proponent of the changes in gardening style, published a description of a *ferme ornée*, literally "ornamental farm." Switzer apparently coined the term, attributing it to the French to provide it a more elevated pedigree.[7] His basic idea was that a working farm, including fields, grazing lands, timber, flower parterres, and vegetable gardens, should be united in a harmonious whole. Switzer was drawing upon

an earlier idea of Joseph Addison. Writing in *Spectator* magazine in 1712, Addison asked, "Why may not a whole estate be thrown into a kind of garden. . . that may turn as much to the profit as the pleasure of the owner?"[8] To create a pretty and productive landscape, Addison and Switzer championed a gradual transition from geometric gardens near the house to more extensive, natural landscapes in the distance. Serpentine walks wound around parterres of box and flowers, and then through groves of trees, past lakes, culminating in vistas of newly mown fields of hay or grazing sheep in pastures.

Switzer experimented with the appearance of the vegetable garden in the *ferme ornée*. He was already familiar with the practical aspects of vegetable gardening since he had published a popular work on how to cultivate a kitchen garden, including a specialized treatise on growing broccoli. For the overall appearance of a vegetable garden, Switzer maintained Quintinie's geometric aesthetic. He departed from Quintinie only in suggesting unusual shapes as opposed to the more prosaic squares. For example, he designed an octagonal vegetable garden, edged in box.[9] Switzer also toyed with the placement of the vegetable garden. He published a plan showing several small vegetable gardens, still geometric, but scattered throughout the grounds and linked by the requisite serpentine paths.[10] Switzer was also aware of the intrinsic visual interest of vegetables. In his practical kitchen garden guide, he asked, "Can the garden afford any thing more delightful to view than those forests of asparagus, artichokes, lettuce, pease, beans and other legumes and edulous plants so different in colour and of such various shapes."[11]

Even with all his ideas about new approaches to the vegetable garden, Switzer affirmed the growing distinction between the landscape and the kitchen gardener. Being a kitchen gardener, even a very skilled kitchen gardener, did not necessarily mean that one could successfully work in this new art of landscape gardening. "The [landscape] gardener bears the same relation to the Kitchen-Gardener that the [landscape] painter does to the House-Painter" is how one eighteenth-century writer put it.[12] William Shenstone, who separated landscape gardening from kitchen gardening, actually constructed the most famous *ferme ornée* in England at Leasowes, his home in Warwickshire. Yet, in the very popular description of Leasowes that was published the year after his death, there is no mention of the vegetable garden.[13]

An increasingly wide aesthetic gulf was developing between vegetable gardens and formal gardens that were defined as pastoral landscapes as opposed to parterres. Despite the work of Switzer and other advocates of the *ferme ornée*, the vegetable garden was simply incongruous in a landscape garden, and most landscape designers chose to marginalize it.

At Twickenham, Pope's vegetable garden, which included cabbages that he had written about with pride, was confined to a long narrow strip along the edge of the property, out of the way of his pleasure garden. Lancelot "Capability" Brown (1716–1783),

the most famous creator of landscape gardens, started his career as a kitchen gardener at Lord Cobham's estate at Stowe—a fact often sneered at by his critics when they took exception to the gardens Brown created. William Chambers (1726–1796), in a thinly veiled attack on Brown's work, wrote in his *Dissertation on Oriental Gardening:*

In this island it [landscape gardening] is abandoned to kitchen gardeners, well skilled in the culture of sallads, but little acquainted with the principles of Ornamental Gardening. It cannot be expected that men uneducated and doomed by their condition to waste the vigor of life

FIG. 2-2
Though known as a *ferme ornée*, Marie Antoinette's rustic village on the grounds of Versailles was really a *ferme de jeu*, a "play farm." In 1783, the queen had a Norman village constructed around a lake where she spent a good deal of her time, entertaining and occasionally playing dairy maid. While the exteriors were all rough-hewn timber and plaster, the interiors were sumptuously appointed with every luxury. In keeping with this elaborate pretense, the vegetable gardens were designed not so much for function but as a beautiful picturesque feature in her faux landscape.
© Gail Mooney

in hard labour, should ever go so far in so refined, so difficult a pursuit.[14]

Chambers had traveled to China and considered the gardens there to be the epitome of ornamental gardening, combining art and nature. He was so taken with the idea that he erected a pagoda in the garden of the Princess of Wales at Kew. For Brown's part, he seems to have been ambivalent about the kitchen garden. When he redesigned the grounds at Blenheim Palace in Oxfordshire, he ignored its walled kitchen garden, but at Burghley House in Lincolnshire, he demolished a terraced vegetable garden near the house and planted it with trees.[15]

From the mid-eighteenth century on, garden writers and landscape designers spoke only rarely of vegetable gardens, described by one author as a "blemish in the prospect."[16] Even the most skilled practitioners of the day could find little aesthetic appeal in the vegetable garden. In 1803, Humphrey Repton wrote in his influential treatise, *Observations on the Theory and Practice of Landscape Gardening*, "If a kitchen-garden consists of such unsightly crops . . . there will be little inducement to make it one of the visible appendages of a place."[17] As these ideas matured in England, one man in America was grappling with the difficulties posed by the vegetable garden in a landscape. When Thomas Jefferson sought to create a *ferme ornée* at Monticello, he, too, was stymied by how to ornament his vegetable garden.

No occupation is so delightful to me as the culture of the earth, and no culture comparable to that of the garden. . . . Under a total want of demand except for our family table, I am still devoted to the garden. But though an old man,

I am but a young gardener.

Thomas Jefferson to Charles Willson Peale, August 20, 1811

Certainly the most famous Colonial American vegetable garden is the one on the grounds of Thomas Jefferson's Monticello near Charlottesville, Virginia.[18] Carefully restored from historical documentation and archaeological research, visitors can now see Jefferson's scientifically arranged square beds that cling to the side of a hill. This beautiful vegetable garden is a fitting memorial to its creator. Jefferson delighted in his mountain-top garden, even though his sense of duty to a nascent nation often kept him from his beloved Monticello for years on end.

In 1770, Thomas Jefferson was a twenty-seven-year-old successful lawyer and erstwhile planter. In that year, he moved into his new home that was 876 feet above sea level and far from a good source of water. Nonetheless, he immediately began to plant a vegetable garden along the hillside. When he was able to escape from the demands of his law practice, Jefferson maintained detailed notations about what he planted, the date it sprouted (if it did), and when it was harvested. The earliest notes

arc erratic, but he lists asparagus, artichokes, and peas among other vegetables. Peas would be a constant refrain at Monticello, including a friendly rivalry with a neighbor to see who could bring the earliest peas to the table.[19] The importance of Jefferson's vegetable garden can be seen in his detailed notes from 1777. During the upheaval of the American Revolution, he still took time to note the location and timing of each planting of purple cabbage, *broccolini*, lettuce, radishes, coleworts, Russian curled greens (kales), endive, red mustard, cucumbers, lima beans, Irish potatoes, and spinach.[20]

Over time, Jefferson's vegetable garden expanded to become one thousand feet long, as his slaves carved a level terrace from the side of a mountain. The excavated stone was used to construct a twelve-foot-high retaining wall with fig trees planted at the base. Jefferson eventually organized the garden

FIG. 3-5
Monticello, Virginia
The view from the grassy lawn shows the oval flowerbeds, tended by Jefferson's granddaughters, as well as the restored façade of Monticello.
Monticello/Thomas Jefferson Foundation, Inc

FIG. 3-6
Aerial view of the gardens at Monticello
Monticello/Thomas Jefferson Foundation, Inc.

into twenty-four square beds. Plants were grouped together in beds based on which part of the plant was consumed. For example, leafy vegetables like cabbage and lettuce were grown together, as were root vegetables like carrots and onions. His scientific disposition was also seen in his constant desire to try new vegetables and new varieties. He was an early champion of the tomato, and several of his daughter Martha's tomato recipes have survived. He also experimented with sesame, okra, eggplant, and sweetpotatoes. Despite the size of his garden, Jefferson was also reliant on the produce from his slaves' vegetable gardens. He regularly purchased extra fruits and vegetables from them.

Monticello's vegetable garden was a labor of love for Jefferson, who continually refined it over thirty years until he retired from public service. When he could not be at Monticello, he followed the gardens' progress through his daughters' letters and, later, through those of his granddaughters. However, the vegetable garden was only part of his grand scheme for horticulture at Monticello, both as a working farm and in its ornamental landscape. Though he had helped foment a revolution against English rule, the English style of gardening was to be his inspiration at Monticello.

From 1784 to 1789, Jefferson served as ambassador to France. In June 1785, he visited Versailles, hiring a chair to be carried around the extensive grounds.[21] He does not mention whether he visited what remained of Quintinie's *potager*, but surely he must have. Intrigued by the vegetables grown in France, Jefferson sent thirty different varieties back

to America in 1786.[22] Nonetheless, while he was impressed by Le Nôtre's creations and perhaps could sympathize with King Louis's love of fresh peas, the more significant inspiration for his designs at Monticello came from the gardens he visited in England in 1786. He made notes about sixteen gardens, using Thomas Whatley's *Observations in Modern Gardening* as his guide.[23] Jefferson found Hampton Court Palace in Richmond to be "old-fashioned" with the "clipt yews grown wild." He noted the inscription on the obelisk memorial to Pope's mother at Twickenham. He thought the Doric temple at Painshill "beautiful." Jefferson also admired the small classical temple at Chiswick House, but noted that one obelisk had an "ill effect" and another, placed in the middle of a pond, was "useless." In addition to commenting on garden ornaments, Jefferson studied the kitchen gardens at various sites, noting how large they were and how many people were needed for their upkeep. Leasowes was already past its prime, and Jefferson noted that "this is not even an ornamented farm—it is only a grazing farm with a path round it, here and there a seat of board, rarely anything better." However, one senses his approval at Woburn Farm in Surrey, where he records "four people [laborers] to the farm, four to the pleasure garden, four to the kitchen garden. All are intermixed, the pleasure garden being merely a highly ornamented walk through and round the divisions of the farm and kitchen garden."[24]

When Jefferson returned to the United States, political duties again kept him away from Monticello,

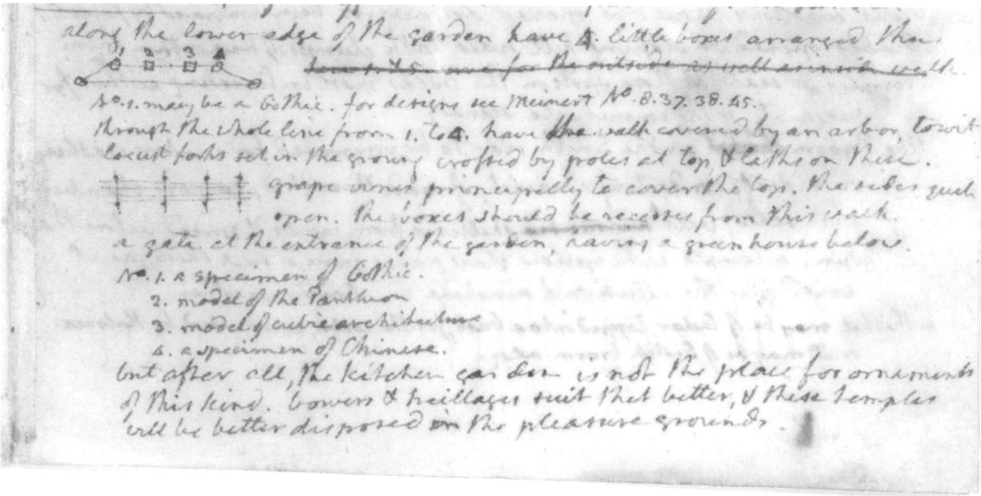

FIG. 3-7
Detail of figure 3-8 (opposite)
showing the excerpt transcribed.

but he was able to make some improvements to his farm. He was clearly taken with the idea of a *ferme ornée* and made specific reference to the term in an 1808 memorandum to his farm manager. Jefferson requested that a series of experimental plots be arranged "into a *ferme ornée* by interspersing occasionally the attributes of a garden."[25] Unfortunately, what those attributes were was not specified, but the organization of his farm shows the influence of the *ferme ornée* ideal. For the overall layout, he divided the grounds into a series of zones based on agricultural activity. Each zone was encircled by a road that Jefferson called a "roundabout," which allowed him to inspect his holdings. On top of the mountain was the house with a grassy lawn, serpentine drive, and oval flowerbeds, which were under the special care of his granddaughters. Below the house were the vegetable garden, orchards, vineyards, and woodlands. Finally, fields formed an outer ring.[26] Because of the drop in elevation, all components of the farm were linked by the panoramic vista of the house on top of the mountain.

While his farm was well organized, Jefferson also wanted to ornament it. According to his surviving notes, he spent many hours doodling over possibilities. The water supply would not allow a large tranquil lake, but he had speculated about building a picturesque, cascading waterfall down one side of the mountain. Jefferson eventually settled for a smaller fishpond on the house grounds. He pondered an elaborate maze of Scotch broom and the placement of a mount, a raised platform for viewing the grounds. Jefferson also wanted to add ornamental buildings to his landscape and carefully copied a plan of the temple at Chiswick and a Chinese building described by William Chambers.[27] However, his vegetable garden became a challenge to ornament.

As noted, Jefferson's English contemporaries usually wrote of the vegetable garden as, if not ugly, certainly visually uninteresting. Jefferson, on the other hand, seems to have been more sensitive to the ornamental qualities of his vegetable garden. He planted alternating rows of green, white, and purple broccoli and white and purple eggplant to enliven the neat, square beds. He contrasted the texture of tomato with okra planted along the edge of the bed. Although he thought the 'Caracalla' or 'Snail Bean' was the most beautiful bean in the world, he also planted 'Scarlet Runner Bean' as a colorful arbor along the garden walk. Yet when Jefferson attempted to combine his English-inspired landscape garden with his French-inspired vegetable garden, he reached an impasse.

In a memorandum to himself, probably from around 1804 when he was living in Washington, Jefferson decided to place four small buildings or temples along the edge of the vegetable garden. Each would represent a different style: Cubic, Greek, Gothic, and Chinese. He planned to connect the temples with a grapevine arbor, though at the very bottom of the page, he notes his doubts: "But after all, the kitchen garden is not the place for ornament of this kind, bowers and trellages suit that better and these temples will be better disposed in the pleasure grounds."[28]

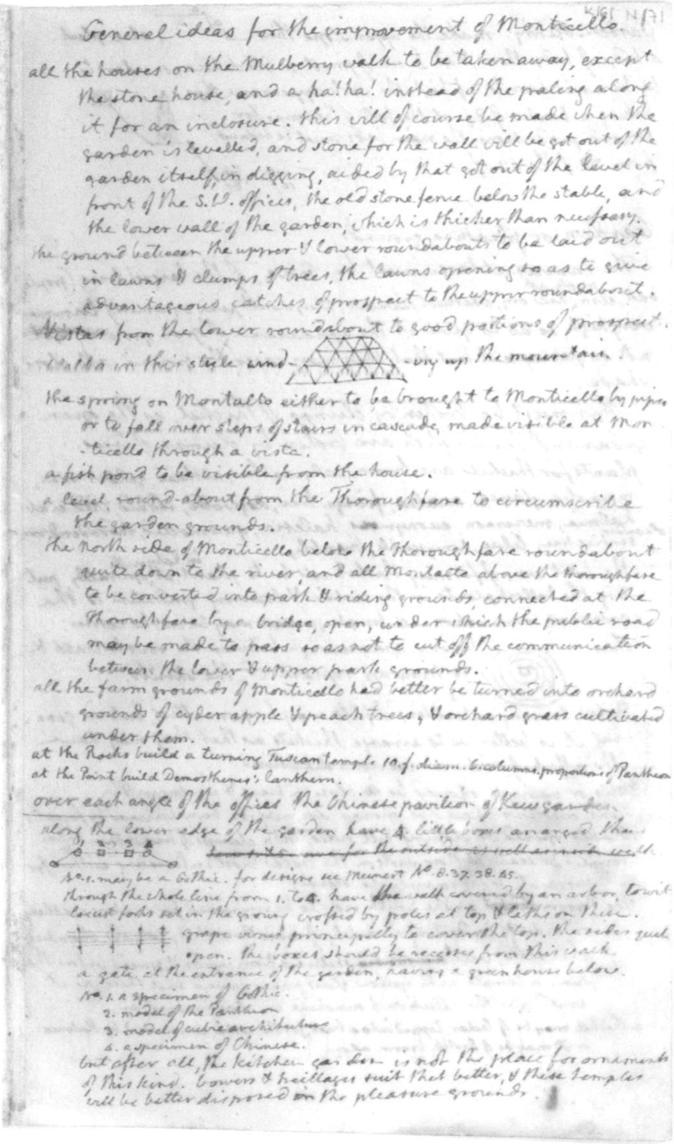
General ideas for the improvement of Monticello.
all the houses on the Mulberry walk to be taken away, except the stone house, and a ha! ha! instead of the paling along it for an inclosure. this will of course be made when the garden is levelled, and stone for the wall will be got out of the garden itself in digging, aided by that got out of the level in front of the S.W. offices, the old stone fence below the stable, and the lower wall of the garden, which is thicker than necessary.
the ground between the upper & lower roundabouts to be laid out in lawns & clumps of trees, the lawns opening so as to give advantageous catches of prospect to the upper roundabout.
Vistas from the lower roundabout to good portions of prospect.
walks in this style wind- -ing up the mountain.
the spring on Montalto either to be brought to Monticello by pipes or to fall over steps of stairs in cascade, made visible at Monticello through a vista.
a fish pond to be visible from the house.
a level round-about from the Thoroughfare to circumscribe the garden grounds.
the North side of Monticello below the Thoroughfare roundabout quite down to the river, and all Montalto above the thoroughfare to be converted into park & riding grounds, connected at the Thoroughfare by a bridge, open, under which the public road may be made to pass so as not to cut off the communication between the lower & upper park grounds.
all the farm grounds of Monticello had better be turned into orchard grounds of cyder apple & peach trees, & orchard grass cultivated under them.
at the Rocks build a turning Tuscan temple 10 f. diam. 6 columns, proportions of Pantheon
at the Point build Demosthenes's Lanthern.
over each angle of the offices the Chinese pavilion of Kew garden.
along the lower edge of the garden have 4 little boxes arranged thus
No. 1. may be a Gothic. for designs see Meinert No. 8.37.38.45. through the whole line from 1. to 4. have the walk covered by an arbor, to wit locust forks set in the ground crossed by poles at top & lathes on these.
grape vines principally to cover the top. the sides quite open. the boxes should be recessed from this walk.
a gate at the entrance of the garden, having a green house below.
No. 1. a specimen of Gothic
2. model of the Pantheon
3. model of cubic architecture
4. a specimen of Chinese.
but after all, the kitchen garden is not the place for ornaments of this kind. bowers & treillages suit that better, & these temples will be better disposed in the pleasure grounds.

FIG. 3-8
"General ideas for the improvement of Monticello," c. 1804

Jefferson's notes about his gardens at Monticello clearly show how the English landscape style of gardening influenced his thoughts. He planned to put in a "ha-ha!," a lawn "to give advantageous catches of prospect," and a fish pond.

along the lower edge of the garden have 4 little boxes arranged thus No. 1 may be a Gothic for designs see Meinert No 8.37.38.45 through the whole line from 1. to 4. have the walk covered by an arbor, to wit locust _ [illegible] set in the growing crossed by poles at top and lathes on these

Grape vine principally to cover the top, the sides just open. The boxes should be recessed from this work, a gate at the entrance of the garden, having a greenhouse below.

No. 1. A specimen of Gothic
2. model of the Pantheon
3. model of cubic architecture
4. a specimen of Chinese
but after all, the kitchen garden is not the place for ornament of this kind, bowers and trellages suit that better and these temples will be better disposed in the pleasure grounds.

Thomas Jefferson Papers, Massachusetts Historical Society

The restored vegetable garden at the William
Paca House and Garden in Annapolis, Maryland.
Growing beans and peas on vertical frames is
not only a practical adaptation to their growth
habit but also an opportunity to have cascades
of beautiful flowers in the spring.
Courtesy of The Historic Annapolis Foundation

Possibly, without consciously realizing it, Jefferson's
inherent aesthetic sense, influenced by what he had
seen in England, told him that one could not combine high art with the vegetable garden. Perhaps he
also was remembering a phrase in Whatley's book:
*Though a farm and a garden agree in many particulars
connected with extent, yet in style they are the two
extremes. Both indeed are subjects of cultivation; but
cultivation in the one is husbandry; and in the other
decoration: the former is appropriated to profit, the latter to pleasure: fields profusely ornamented do not
retain the appearance of a farm; and an apparent attention to produce obliterates the idea of a garden.*[29]
Simply put, one cannot create an idyllic tableau
amidst the cabbages. Yet the view from the vegetable

garden across the picturesque mountains was too
gorgeous to forgo, so Jefferson built a small pavilion
on the edge of the vegetable garden where he could
sit and read and look out over the countryside.

UNWORTHY OF THE NAME "GARDEN"

Much like Switzer, Jefferson was a prophet in the
wilderness. The idea of vegetable gardens as an
intricate component of a *ferme ornée* landscape did
not catch on in America any more than it did in
England. J. C. Loudon, writing in 1834, stated the
case clearly: "The kitchen garden is not to be considered as having any beauty as such; . . . [It] should
be so situated as to be convenient to, and, at the
same time, be concealed from, the house."[30]
Professional gardeners recognized the necessity of a
vegetable garden, but they saw no beauty in it.

This condemnation was not universal, however.
The vegetable garden always had its apologists.
Writing in 1829, critic William Cobbett considered
it in the "most miserable taste to seek to poke away
the kitchen-garden. . . . If well managed, nothing is
more beautiful than the kitchen-garden. . . .
Therefore, I see no reason for placing the kitchen-
garden in some out-of-the-way place, . . . as if it
were a mere necessary evil, and unworthy of being
viewed by the owner."[31] Cobbett was the exception,
not the rule.

Moreover, while *ferme ornée* may not have been
very popular in America, landscape and ornamental
gardening were. In 1848, Andrew Jackson Downing,

FIG. 3-10
Reconstructed after archaeological excavation, the pavilion in the vegetable garden
provides the modern visitor with the same panorama that Jefferson enjoyed.
Smithsonian Institution, Archives of American Gardens, Garden Club of America
Collection, photo: Eleanor C. Weller, 1984

FIG. 3-11

Pitney Farm, Edward Kranich, c. 1860

Approximately forty years after William Cobbett's apologia for the kitchen garden, the Pitney family commissioned this painting of their homestead in Mendham, New Jersey. Carefully fenced off from the cows, the vegetable garden is a surprisingly important element in the visual composition of the painting.

The arbor and edged beds echo Cobbett's statements well. The Pitney family continues to live on the farm, and the backbone of the vegetable garden is still present, though now dominated by roses.
Courtesy of Mr. and Mrs. J. Duncan Pitney

one of the earliest American landscape designers, published a gardening magazine in which he noted the popularity of ornamental gardening as striking proof of the increasing refinement of his young nation.[32] In the same volume of that magazine, George Kidd, a professional gardener, noted that the kitchen garden's "close proximity with the mansion mars the effect of a fine landscape; and the necessarily tedious mode of cultivating it, is by no means in accordance with the energetic character of the Americans."[33] The case was more forcibly made ten years later by gardener Edward Kemp, who aptly summed up the change in the perception of the vegetable garden:

Some gardens are, moreover, so contracted, or of such a peculiar shape, that the appropriation of any part of them to vegetables or fruits appears quite inconsistent with the attainment of any kind of beauty in the ornamental portions. And, in such instances, the kitchen department *may very properly be omitted. A mere scrap or corner of kitchen garden, which only serves to mar the general design, can afford no real pleasure; . . . If the ground lies entirely in front of the principal windows, and is but narrow, a kitchen garden would seem inadmissible, in point of taste; the front of a house appearing to demand only ornamental and pleasurable accompaniments.*[34]

By the turn of the century the transformation was complete. Vegetable gardens were excluded from refined gardening. In 1912, H. G. Dwight wrote

in the *Atlantic Monthly,* "As for vegetables, I do not consider a plot of ground devoted to them worthy of the honorable name of garden." This is not to imply that people stopped vegetable gardening. They did not. Vegetable gardening remained a popular pastime and a practical necessity for many Americans. Instead, vegetable gardens had lost their last shred of aesthetic appeal. This disjuncture between vegetable and pleasure garden is clearly illustrated by the difficulties that the Lane family had in finding a place for their much-prized vegetable garden at their estate, Chimneys, in the early part of the twentieth century.

FIG. 3-12
The vegetable and herb garden at the Boscobel Restoration in Garrison, New York, c. 1983 States Morris Dyckman, a Loyalist during the Revolutionary War, built Boscobel during the first decade of the nineteenth century. Dyckman died before the house was completed, but his descendants ran Boscobel as a working farm for nearly a century. After falling into disrepair, the house was eventually dismantled and moved to its current location, where it houses a fine collection of Federal period antiques. The local garden club maintains the reconstructed vegetable and herb garden designed by Frederick Strayer, the director of Boscobel Restoration. While Strayer was influenced by early nineteenth-century garden plans, the vegetable garden was designed not to mimic the working vegetable garden of the original farm, but to complement the landscape and formal gardens created by Innocenti and Webel. Period features such as the woven-straw bee skep enhance the historic look.
Courtesy of Boscobel Restoration, Inc., Garrison, New York

4

A VEGETABLE GARDEN CONUNDRUM
Chimneys

*When I marry I'm going to push all the
vegetables over the fence
into the field and have nothing but flowers here,
and I'm going to buy bulbs and roses by the hundred
instead of by sixes*

The Gardener (Mabel Osgood Wright),
The Garden of a Commuter's Wife, 1949

Chimneys in Manchester, Massachusetts, was the family home of sculptor Katharine Lane Weems, best known for creating the rhinoceros that stands guard before the Biological Laboratories at Harvard University and a set of frolicking dolphins at the New England Aquarium in Boston. Weems was no struggling artist, though. Her father, Gardiner Martin Lane, was a wealthy financier who once served as president of the Museum of Fine Arts, Boston. For their only surviving child, Katharine's parents provided a life of privilege. Nothing (including the requisite childhood Shetland pony) was denied her and she could have easily progressed from pampered child to debutante to society wife. Certainly those were her mother's expectations, but Katharine wanted to be an artist. At eighteen,

she began serious instruction in drawing and sculpture. She eventually converted the stable at Chimneys into her studio and devoted her life to her sculpture, not marrying her long-time friend, Carrington Weems, until she was in her mid-forties.

Constructed between 1902 and 1914, Chimneys was the family's summer home. Because Katharine's parents were fond of open fireplaces, the house had seven chimneys, which inspired its name. As befitting their social standing, the Lanes contracted with the most prestigious firm of landscape architects in the country, the Olmsted Brothers, to design the gardens and grounds.

In 1902, Frederick Law Olmsted Jr. visited with Mr. and Mrs. Lane at the construction site of their new home to discuss the ornamental garden design. The Lanes initially wanted an "informal" or "landscape" garden, but Olmsted was opposed to that idea. Perhaps sharing William Chambers's opinion, Olmsted thought the approach was "too subtle" for the average gardener. Instead, he proffered his theory of garden design:

In a regular garden enclosed by a boundary which no one can pass without recognizing, you are very much freer to grow whatever you wish for itself, for the individual

beauty of its flowers or foliage, and you do not run the risk of having your gardener, in his mistaken zeal, extend the garden treatment by driblets to the areas that should be controlled by other motives.[1]

The garden design presented by the Olmsted firm, and finally agreed upon by the Lanes, was typical of turn-of-the-century Italianate gardens. Behind the house, an elevated, semicircular piazza provided a dramatic prospect overlooking the sea and a nearby island. From the piazza, a walkway led along the cliff's edge to the flower and water gardens, the true centerpiece of the design. The dense plantings on either side of the walk opened to a broad green terrace, rimmed by a white, ornamental fence and a pergola. In the center, a circular pool within a square perimeter was framed by white stone. The effect was an architecturally inspired stage for potted plants and flowerbeds, accented by white fences and pool borders that provided the clean boundaries Olmsted desired. The overall effect was very successful, and the Lanes' garden was frequently mentioned with approval in popular garden magazines and guidebooks for more than thirty years.[2] The articles often noted the effect of seclusion and privacy in the garden, which was located away from the house and shielded by dense plantings and the ornamental fence.

The formal garden was not the only one at Chimneys, however. The vegetable garden is regularly mentioned in correspondence with the Olmsted firm, and it was actually the first garden planted on the property in 1902. The surviving garden books of the Lane and Weems families, which provide seventy years of vegetable garden history, describe the varieties ordered and where they were planted.[3] From the books one can discern how important the vegetable garden was to the family. Mrs. Lane regularly ordered more than fifty varieties of vegetables, patronizing both American and European merchants. She tried new vegetables with varying degrees of success. For example, both okra and celeriac were ordered only once. 'Fordhook Lima Beans,' on the other hand, were a constant fixture in her garden. A comparison of her orders to the seed catalogs of the period reveals that Mrs. Lane was much swayed by illustrated varieties as well as any variety named for a member of a European royal family.

Mrs. Lane took her vegetables seriously. She exhibited vegetables at local horticultural shows and won prizes for her cabbages several years running.[4]

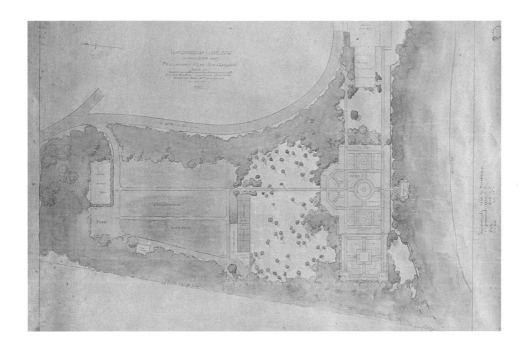

FIG. 4-3
Olmsted Brothers' plan of the gardens
at Chimneys, January 1906
The serpentine drive to the house is located at
the top of the plan. Notice the proposed dense
plantings between it and the vegetable garden.
The "wild" area between the formal garden on
the right and the vegetable garden on the left
(shaded purple) served as a visual transition
between the two gardens.
Smithsonian Institution, Archives of American
Gardens, The Chimneys Collection

FIG. 4-4
The view from Chimneys' piazza, 1942
Smithsonian Institution, Archives of American
Gardens, Garden Club of America Collection

FIG. 4-6
Katharine Lane by the center pool in the formal garden at Chimneys, 1911. Smithsonian Institution, Archives of American Gardens, Garden Club of America Collection

(ABOVE) FIG. 4-5
Italianate gardens and pool at Chimneys, 1920s. Smithsonian Institution, Archives of American Gardens, Garden Club of America Collection

FIG. 4-7
This 1942 photograph is the only image of Chimneys' vegetable gardens. It was probably taken to show off the lovely blooms of the flower borders as much as to highlight the ripening produce. Smithsonian Institution, Archives of American Gardens, Garden Club of America Collection

Moreover, Chimneys' vegetable garden was not a small patch that provided the occasional head of lettuce for the table. It covered the same acreage as the formal garden and produced enough vegetables to feed the entire household. In a 1947 letter to the Olmsted firm, Mrs. Lane notes that she wanted to simplify the formal garden because of the "limited" staff; only three men then worked on the grounds. At the same time, she wanted to scale back the vegetable garden to feed eight or nine people, which presumably included Mrs. Lane, the Weems, and a reduced household staff.[5] Unfortunately, there are no indications of how large the staff was in the heyday of Chimneys.

After Mrs. Lane's death, responsibility for the gardens fell to Carrington Weems, who was not as experimental as his mother-in-law. Though he ordered the same varieties of vegetables year after year, he was certainly interested in the vegetable garden. In exhaustive correspondence with the head gardener, he gave detailed instructions as to what exactly should be planted where and when. Katharine's autobiography mentions that her husband particularly looked forward to the fresh produce from the vegetable garden each summer.[6]

For all the attention given to it, the vegetable garden was not meant to be seen. Located to the north of the formal garden, below a steep hill, it was beside the serpentine drive that led to the house. From the first, the Lanes wanted the vegetable garden hidden from sight. In an April 27, 1903, letter Mr. Lane made his concerns explicit:

When I was last at Manchester I looked at the plantings

FIG. 4-8
Formal terrace gardens at Chimneys, 1920s
Terraced steps, with their rough stone masonry and rock plants, provide an aesthetic transition from the Italianate garden on the top terrace to the vegetable garden terrace below. In this photograph, the vegetable garden is behind the viewer. Smithsonian Institution, Archives of American Gardens, Garden Club of America Collection

between the proposed avenue [driveway into Chimneys] and the vegetable garden. It seems to me that it will be necessary to plant a row or rows of something much higher that will grow more quickly than the small pines that have recently got out. It is desirable that the vegetable garden be pretty well screened from the view of passersby in carriages. The pines recently set out, will not be high enough to make a satisfactory screen for many years, and I am now too old to wait many years.[7]
In addition to the pines, the vegetable garden was eventually shielded from the formal garden by a tall, ornamental fence. Chimneys may have shared many features with a working farm, but the idea of *ferme ornée* had long since passed from fashion. This was the beginning of the modern era, and while one might plant 'Telephone Peas' or 'Telegraph

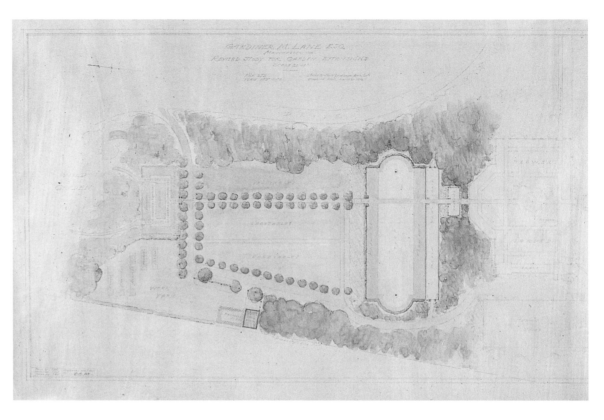

Cucumbers,' the vegetable garden itself was simply an old-fashioned, unseemly necessity.

The desire to hide the vegetable garden from the formal garden became even more of a concern when the Lanes decided to expand the vegetable and cutting flower gardens. The best way to expand was to cut into the slope that led up to the Italianate garden.[8] However, at the turn of the century, it was unsuitable to have the vegetable garden directly abut the pleasure garden. In a 1907 letter to Mr. Lane, the Olmsted firm offered the following observations:

The other matter, that of a suitable connection between the flower and vegetable gardens has resolved itself, in our minds, into two rather similar plans both of which we are sending you. They differ in that one recommends a row of fruit trees on either side of the walk and the other shows flower beds, which could be edged with some attractive vegetable.[9]

The final choice was to use flowers, not attractive vegetables, to edge the beds. While no photographs are extant that indicate the exact relationship between the vegetable and formal gardens, a surviving image of the vegetable garden shows the success in minimizing the impact of its appearance. Trellised arches framed the central walk at either end so that one's eye was pulled straight through the vegetable garden. The tall, colorful flowers in the border beds shield the rows of vegetables so that

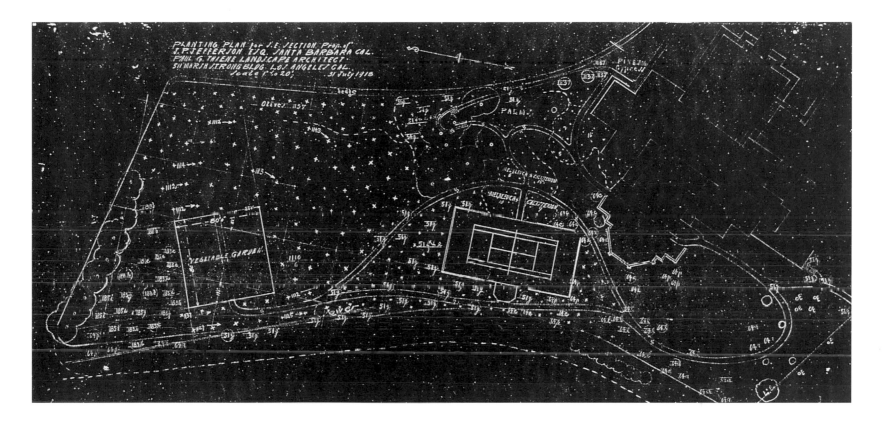

FIG. 4-10
Planting plan for Miraflores, Paul G. Thiene, July 31, 1918
Since 1951, the estate of Miraflores in Santa Barbara, California,
has housed the Music Academy of the West summer school and
festival. In 1918, however, Miraflores was still a private residence.
Its vegetable garden was apparently located at the very corner of
the estate, shielded behind trees.
Used by permission of the Music Academy of the West, Santa
Barbara, California

FIG. 4-11
A planting of shaped evergreens hides the vegetable garden from the
oval formal garden at Gross' Coate, near Easton, Maryland, c. 1940.
Courtesy of The Historical Society of Talbot County, Easton,
Maryland, photo: H. Robins Hollyday

FIG. 4-12

At Rohallion in Rumson, New Jersey, 1910–1920s, a tall box hedge hid the large vegetable garden that fed the estate. Landscape architect Nathan Barrett designed a pastoral vista that highlighted the formal aspects of the landscape. While the vegetable garden was important for its produce, and the family took pride in showing the vegetables at local agricultural shows, the garden could not be allowed to spoil the view.
Smithsonian Institution, Archives of American Gardens, Garden Club of America Collection

FIG. 4-13

Between 1898 and 1902, W. P. Brown built an impressive home in Coffeyville, Kansas. It included a formal terraced garden that led down to a small pond. The vegetable garden and greenhouse were off to one side. In her diary, Nancy Kilgore Brown tells of going to the greenhouse nearly every day for fresh vegetables. "January 12, 1908: I worked in the greenhouse this morning quite a little time. Brought some flowers up to the house and some lettuce, radishes and onions. The greenhouse is such a pleasure this winter to me."
Courtesy of Coffeyville Historical Society, Inc.

at an initial glance it is difficult to see a vegetable garden at all.

Olmsted's letter shows the aesthetic evolution that the vegetable garden had undergone. It was no longer considered formal. The Olmsteds could have looked back to Quintinie for a geometric aesthetic that complemented the clear, crisp architectural lines of the flower garden. Instead, the only way to resolve the conflict in their minds was to hide the vegetable garden, behind trees, fences, and flower bordered paths. The vegetable garden might be functional, but it could no longer be ornamental.

The story of the vegetable garden at Chimneys is not a unique one in the early part of the twentieth century. Throughout the country, vegetable gardens of large estates were tucked away in corners or surrounded by trees and tall fences. Photographic collections from this period include hundreds of images of formal gardens, but surviving photographs of vegetable gardens are extremely rare. If it were not for blueprints and occasional mention in letters and diaries, one would be hard-pressed to know that vegetable gardens ever existed on these estates. At the same time that vegetable gardens were being hidden away because they lacked visual appeal, vegetables themselves were making a splashy comeback, literally. Nineteenth- and twentieth-century artists proclaimed the vegetable still life as the preferred vehicle to express their vision of beauty.

5

THE VEGETABLE STILL LIFE

*Was not a bunch of carrots, carefully studied
and painted naively, in the personal manner in
which one sees it, worth just as much as the eternal
ham of the École des Beaux-Arts . . .
The day is coming when a single carrot would
signify a revolution.*

Émile Zola, *L'Œuvre*, 1886

From the mosaics of ancient Pompeii to the tomato soup cans of pop artist Andy Warhol, vegetables have been subjects of Western art for the last two thousand years. The vegetable still life has been both scorned and praised. At times it has been considered mundane, prosaic, and lacking in any artistic merit. At other times, it has been considered the perfect vehicle to explore new techniques and artistic visions. To this day, the form, color, and shape of vegetables consistently lure artists, regardless of their school or chosen medium.

Around 1650, Europeans began to use the term "still life" to refer to paintings that, as the name implies, sat still. For these early still lifes, artists often chose fruits and flowers because they carried symbolic meaning that imparted an extra significance to the composition. For example, lilies brought to mind Christ's passion, while the entirety of original sin could be summed up in a single, well-painted apple. Vegetables, for the most part, carried fewer symbolic connotations. Artists could contrast expensive vegetables, like artichokes or asparagus, with the humble peasant fare of cabbages and onions in an implied critique of luxurious living. More often, though, vegetables were simply part of larger compositions depicting kitchen or market scenes.

As still life painting matured, artists became less concerned with symbolic meaning and more concerned with accurate representation of their subjects. Careful attention was paid to texture, color, and modeling. Backgrounds were simplified to focus attention on the subject of the painting. The composition was brought to the front of the picture plane, even projecting beyond it, in an attempt to fool the observer's eye. Artists found new sources of inspiration in the natural world. In the Netherlands, Jan Brueghel the Elder (1568–1625) painted massive bouquets of flowers, often scouring the countryside to find rare specimens. In Italy, Michelangelo Merisi da Caravaggio (1573–1610) rendered baskets of fruits with an intensity of focus that had rarely

FIG. 5-1
Head of a Cabbage with Insects, Netherlandish, early 17th century
An increased attention to artistic detail and a broadening appreciation of the natural world led to the juxtaposition of butterflies and a head of cabbage in this seventeenth-century painting. National Gallery of Art, Washington, D.C., Rosenwald Collection, photo: © 2001 Board of Trustees

FIG. 5-2
Quince, Cabbage, Melon and Cucumber,
Juan Sánchez Cotán, c. 1602
San Diego Museum of Art (Gift of Anne R. and Amy Putnam)

been seen before. However, in Spain, Carthusian monk Juan Sánchez Cotán (1560–1627) found his inspiration in vegetables.

Cotán's paintings are set in kitchen cooling niches, or *cantareros,* the stark outlines of which provide a clean background for the vegetables. In *Quince, Cabbage, Melon and Cucumber* (c. 1602), no brushstrokes distract from the precision with which he renders the tattered edges of the cabbage or the individual warts of the cucumber. However, the realism is subservient to a greater need for mathematical order. The fruits and vegetables are arranged in a parabolic arc that flows in three dimensions. The cabbage projects ever so slightly in front of the quince. The slice of melon serves as the transition from the spherical forms to the cucumber, which protrudes farthest out of the picture frame. In other paintings, Cotán more explicitly utilized the underlying geometry of the vegetables. For example, he was fond of the delicate curve of cardoon stems.[1]

In the eighteenth century, the Romantics idealized art and constructed a ranked typology of art forms. Still life painting, and vegetable still lifes in particular, suffered in comparison to portrait and landscape painting. Gerard de Lairesse, an art critic of the period, noted that vegetables were unacceptable subjects for paintings because they excited no noble sentiments: "Cabbage, carrots, and turnips, codfish, salmon, herring, smelts, and such-like . . . he who is pleased with them may seek them in the Markets."[2] The artistic contest between portrait and still life painters is well illustrated in a single family of painters—the Peales.

FIG. 5-3
Still Life: Balsam Apple and Vegetables, James Peale, 1820s
The Metropolitan Museum of Art, Maria DeWitt Fund, 1939,
photo: © 1993 The Metropolitan Museum of Art

The patriarch of the Peale dynasty was Charles Willson Peale (1741–1827). Philadelphia was his home, but he traveled throughout the colonies and the nascent United States, painting many well-known portraits of Revolutionary War leaders. Peale had little time for delicate artistic sensibilities. Commissions for painting portraits were his livelihood, and he had a large extended family to feed. Not only did he train his brothers, children, nieces, and nephews as professional artists, but he also named four of his sons after Renaissance painters (Raphaelle, Rembrandt, Titian, and Rubens). Given their names, it is hardly surprising that the sons followed in their father's footsteps. Rembrandt (1778–1840) painted portraits, and Titian Ramsay (1799–1885), the youngest child, was known for illustrations in natural history texts. Rubens (1784–1865), who suffered from poor eyesight, served as director of the family museum in Philadelphia, though he did take up painting in the last decade of his life.

Raphaelle (1774–1825), on the other hand, was a near constant source of worry and disappointment to his father. Not only did he indulge in an intemperate lifestyle, but he also preferred to paint still lifes. To some degree his father's concerns were practical. Still life paintings were common ornaments in fashionable drawing rooms and libraries, but they did not command the high price of commissioned portraiture. Raphaelle's paintings of fruit, cakes, and wine decanters were beautifully executed and admired by his contemporaries, but they never afforded him a living. Charles recognized that Raphaelle was a gifted painter but always believed that his son was not living up to his potential. Charles repeatedly admonished him to apply his skills to portrait painting, noting in one letter, "With such talents of exact imitation, your portraits ought to be more excellent."[3] The disdain that Charles felt for still life painting was rooted in the commonly held prejudice that it was the art of the novice, "the ordinary soldiers in art's army." As he put it: "The art of painting portraits cannot be attained without a vast deal of practice, the artist must love the art, or he will not succeed to perfection. It is not like the painting of still life; the painting of objects that have no motion, which any person of tolerable genius, with some application may acquire."[4] One can only imagine his father's disapproving comments if, instead of painting refined delicacies, Raphaelle had chosen to focus on mundane cabbages, carrots, and turnips. One member of the Peale clan did paint vegetables, though apparently not until Charles was very old.

James Peale (1749–1831), Charles's youngest brother, is best known today for his miniature watercolor portraits painted on ivory. Sometime after 1825 James painted a series of vegetable still lifes and exhibited them in 1827 (the year Charles died) and 1829. His early still life efforts were obviously influenced by Raphaelle's work, but the vegetables, never a popular subject with his nephew, allowed James to show much more of an individual style.[5] The composition is looser than the precise geometry of Raphaelle's work. The colors are more vivid and the subjects less idealized. More importantly, in *Still Life: Balsam Apple and Vegetables* (c. 1820s), one can clearly see the artist's eye picking out the most interesting vegetables from the garden. Crinkly cabbage, bumpy squash, and a warty balsam apple frame the glazed smoothness of the eggplant. The rupture in the balsam apple reflects the color of the tomatoes. It also imparts a sense of immediacy, as if, in the second before the viewer glimpsed the painting, the balsam apple had just burst open. While James's work clearly shows the possibilities that vegetables could present to a talented artist, most of his contemporaries shared his brother's disdain. The vegetable still life might have continued to slide into obscurity if not for an 1880 painting of asparagus by Édouard Manet (1832–1883).

In the mid- and late nineteenth century, artists who challenged the ideals of the Romantic movement marched behind the unlikely banner of vegetable still lifes. To some degree, it was damning with faint praise. These artists set out to prove that even an uninspiring vegetable could be reclaimed as a worthy subject if painted well. A beautiful work of art came not from the lofty sentiments inspired by the subject, nor from a mere convincing imitation, but from the artist's ability to transmit his vision of it. Vegetables were preferred subjects because they did not distract the viewer with hidden connotations. German artist Max Liebermann (1847–1935) put it this way:

The bunch of asparagus is interesting only because of the way the artist has treated it; . . . in the case of a figure, a head, or a lovely female form—most particularly the latter—it is also the depicted object itself that interests us.[6]

In his watercolor *Cucumber with Leaves* (c. 1880), Manet renders the cucumber with a minimum of brushstrokes. Yet the vegetable is no less engaging than Cotán's precisely rendered one. Émile Zola's carrot revolution had occurred. Still life paintings, even of vegetables, needed no more apologies. Artists could do with them what they chose.

During the early 1900s, artists used the familiar trope to challenge their audience. *Still Life* (c. 1905) by Henri Matisse, for example, gives the viewer no choice but to stop and look again. An initial impression of chaos resolves itself into familiar shapes. The red blob might be a tomato. Perhaps that is asparagus or celery along the side; perhaps not. Matisse provides just enough clues to echo the familiar framework of a vegetable still life while at the same time exploding it with his "beastly" colors.

As students attempt to master form, color, and especially texture, they will always have a place for vegetables in their portfolios. Moreover, in the face of warring artistic sensibilities, vegetable still lifes have proven remarkably resilient, never a dominant theme but always present. In contemplating the true beauty of vegetables, one is most struck by the mature artist who is able to see vegetables anew. Some artists, like Juan Sánchez Cotán and James

Peale, seemed drawn to them and were able to exploit their unique attributes. Where else could one find the glossy, rich purple of an eggplant, the phantom blue-green of leeks, the intricate crinkles of cos lettuce, or the massive presence of a cabbage head? Yet, while artists had reclaimed the vegetable, it would take two cataclysmic world wars to get people thinking again about the ornamental appeal of vegetable gardens.

FIG. 5-6
Eggplant, Carrots, and Tomatoes,
Charles Demuth, 1927
The vegetable still lifes of Charles Demuth (1883–1935) can only be described as carefully nuanced, loving portrayals of their subject. Demuth's earliest paintings were ethereal watercolor flowers. He then turned to stark, cubist industrial landscapes in oil, only to return to watercolors in the 1920s, though this time it was vegetables that repeatedly captured his attention.
Norton Museum of Art, West Palm Beach, Florida, Bequest of R. H. Norton

FIG. 5-7
Summer Vegetables, Howard Norton Cook, 1930
Howard Norton Cook (1901–1980) was associated with the Taos School in New Mexico and is well known for his prints of Southwestern landscapes and Native American dancers. Cook's *Summer Vegetables* illustrates a different approach to vegetables from Demuth's. By rendering his drawing in black and white, the shapes and textures of the vegetables are brought to the fore.
Smithsonian American Art Museum,
Gift of Barbara Latham

SONDRA FRECKELTON AND "HARVEST"

When I first started gardening, I grew vegetables simply to have the greens of the onions and the multihued outer leaves of the cabbage—subject matter for my watercolors. Painting *Harvest*, I was unaware of how much I had learned from the garden, but soon realized that the making of a garden had very much to do with the making of art. The garden taught me the value of "visual rhyme"—the relationship of similar shape, form, and color to create directions and rhythms, the importance of scale, proportion, and placements in both endeavors. Probably a good half of the paintings I've done have my vegetables in them. It reminds me of the old recipe for rabbit stew, "First, catch a rabbit." I guess that planting a seed and working among the plants for months make you really look at the produce with new eyes. There is nothing much more beautiful to me.

Sondra Freckelton, November 2001

Harvest, Sondra Freckelton, 1979
Smithsonian American Art Museum, Gift of the Sara Roby Foundation

FIG. 6-1

Charles Lathrop Pack reviews his "troops" in this c. 1917 cartoon from the *New York Tribune*. While U.S. Department of Agriculture officials may have considered Pack a Napoleon (he was short in stature), there was no denying that he was a master of publicity. Pack enjoyed a good relationship with newspaper editors who popularized the war garden movement.

Reprinted from *The War Garden Victorious*, Charles Lathrop Pack

6

VEGETABLE GARDEN VICTORIOUS

*Indeed, the vegetable of today may be
the flower of tomorrow,
emerging, as it were, from the kitchen into
the drawing room.
For fashions in gardening have often changed,
and continue to change.*

Jean-Marie Putnam, *Gardens for Victory*, 1943

Except for two specific periods in history, vegetable gardens have never really been a topic of national conversation in America. From 1917 to 1919, and again from 1942 to 1946, posters, newspaper and magazine articles, cartoons, radio shows, clubs, and community programs celebrated the contributions of the humble vegetable patch to the war effort. With all of this attention, it is only natural that people also began to consider the ornamental possibilities of their vegetable gardens.

WORLD WAR I AND THE WAR GARDEN

In February 1917, the war in Europe threatened to engulf America. There were rumors of a railroad strike and people began to hoard food. After the price of cabbage went up two thousand percent, the housewives of New York City overturned market stalls and vegetable carts and marched on the mayor's mansion demanding controls on the escalating prices.[1] The riots were eventually quelled, but new fears arose when, on April 6, the United States entered the war and began to mobilize troops.

Following a call from President Woodrow Wilson for Americans to plant vegetable gardens, businessman Charles Lathrop Pack organized the National War Garden Commission. His goal was "to arouse the patriots of America to the importance of putting all idle land to work, to teach them how to do it, and to educate them to conserve by canning and drying all food they could not use while fresh."[2] Americans enthusiastically responded, partially out of fear and partially out of patriotism. The fear came from the possibility of a true food shortage. Many farms were short-handed when their laborers joined the army. Railroads and other

Drawing a direct connection between life on the home front and the outcome of the war, popular posters printed by the War Garden Commission urged families to plant vegetable gardens. These posters showed vegetables going "over the top" of trenches, the kaiser being canned in a Mason jar, and America personified sowing seeds of victory in a furrowed field.

In backyards, front yards, sidewalk verges, railroad rights-of-way, vacant lots, schoolyards, and company lawns, millions of war gardens were planted, perhaps as many as five million in 1918.[4] Looking back, Americans remembered the war gardens of World War I as plowed-up lawns and ripped-up flower beds, planted with nothing but potatoes, which cost more than their produce was worth.[5] While that might sometimes have been the case, most people grew a wide range of vegetables and did not completely abandon planting flowers.[6] There was even some attempt to make war gardens more ornamental by making them look more like formal flower gardens.

In the January 1918 issue of *Garden Magazine*, Iowa landscape architect Leonidas Willing Ramsey wrote an article entitled "Make Your War Garden Attractive." After noting that "last spring and summer every available space was turned into a vegetable garden," he remarked that there was no reason that the vegetable garden should not be attractive, adding that "we too often associate the vegetable garden with the tin can alley and the garbage dump."[7] The exact meaning of that association is, I'm afraid, lost in the mists of time, but it certainly

transportation facilities were devoted to the movement of troops and munitions, making it difficult to transport what food was grown to distant markets. When produce did arrive at its destination, it was certainly more expensive. Growing your own was "Food F.O.B. the Kitchen Door," as the Commission described it.[3]

While eliminating the market middlemen might mean cheaper, fresher food, war gardens also strongly appealed to American patriotism and an inherent need to participate in the war effort.

FIG. 6-3
War garden of Mr. E. S. Burke, Cleveland, Ohio
The Garden Magazine, June 1918

FIG 6-4
Vegetables planted in a former rose garden,
New Haven, Connecticut, c. 1917
Reprinted from *The War Garden Victorious*,
Charles Lathrop Pack

FIG. 6-5
Better known for its Chinese-influenced
pleasure gardens, the kitchen garden at
Chelsea in Muttontown, New York, illustrates well Leonidas Willing Ramsey's idea
of a formal framework. The sundial provides
a central focus in the star-shaped garden
whose paths were bordered by flowers and
fruit trees.
Courtesy Alfred A. Moore, Smithsonian
Institution, Archives of American Gardens,
Garden Club of America Collection, photo:
Samuel Gottscho

implies a certain "seediness" on the part of the vegetable garden. Ramsey's solution was to formalize
the layout of the vegetable garden.

As at Chimneys, the difficulty in applying
"modern" landscape design to the vegetable garden
was a matter of perception—the vegetable garden was
looked upon as informal and rather old-fashioned.
Ramsey recognized that orderly rows of plants
made caring for them easier; however, he felt a formal framework could render the vegetable garden
attractive. He suggested grass walks with some
form of "crisp" edging to divide the vegetable garden into geometric segments: squares, rectangles,
or even circles. These parterres, as he called them,
then could be subdivided as necessary. Flowers
added along the edges or in the corners provided

color and blossoms for the house. Finally, a bird-
bath or sundial at the main intersection of the paths
provided a central focus to the garden. One could
argue that Ramsey had rediscovered the beauty of
the geometric, baroque vegetable garden.
Nevertheless, his final comments leave no doubt
about the ongoing modern perception of the vegetable garden:

*The garden should be handy to the kitchen and yet not
too close to the house. It is needless to say that the garden
should be screened from the view of the public and even
the neighbors, when such an arrangement is possible,
whether the screen be a planting, fence, or a building.*[8]

Three months later, another approach to making the vegetable garden look like a flower garden
appeared in the same magazine. In an article entitled "Flowers for the War Time Garden," Elizabeth
Strang saw no reason to "forgo the pleasure of flowers
in our gardens just because the usual activity is
directed toward food production."[9] She offered five
plans for flower beds in the style of landscape
designer Gertrude Jekyll's drift planting. Writing at
the turn of the century, Jekyll (1843–1932) proposed
planting flowers in large, irregular, naturalistic
masses or drifts, instead of in blocks or rows. She
also suggested a careful attention to color so that
the borders would flow in harmonious progres-
sions.[10] Strang's ideas represent just such a mixed
planting, charted with different examples of color
values. Four plans are composed only of flowers to
border the vegetable garden and to provide a visual
respite while hoeing. However, her last plan for the
"Ultra Patriot" gardener applies Jekyll's ideas to the

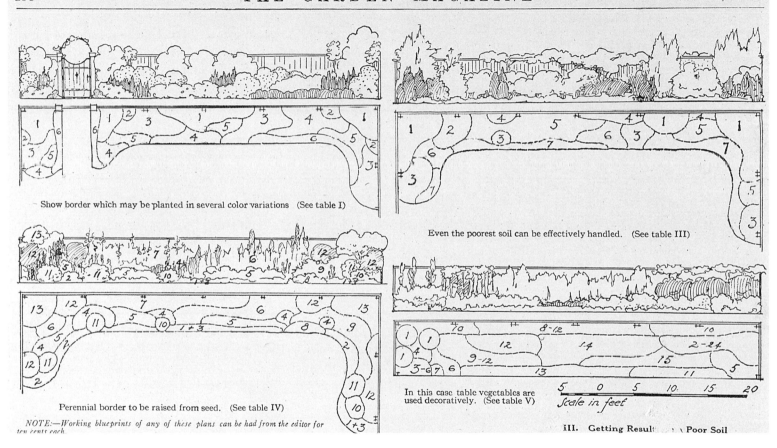

Show border which may be planted in several color variations   (See table I)

Even the poorest soil can be effectively handled.   (See table III)

Perennial border to be raised from seed.   (See table IV)

In this case table vegetables are used decoratively.   (See table V)

Scale in feet

III.   Getting Result   Poor Soil

FIG. 6-6
Vegetable garden layout, *The Garden Magazine,* April 1918
The vegetables that Elizabeth Strang suggested for this garden
layout are listed in figure 6-7.

V. THE USEFUL BORDER

INDEX		DISTANCE APART	COST
HARDY			
1	Rhubarb, 3 plants, or seeds (.05)	2'	$.75
2	Asparagus, 24 plants, or seeds (.05)	12"	.40
3	Horse-radish, 6 plants . . .	12"	.10
4	Peppermint or spearmint, 1 plant		.10
5	Sage, seeds	2'	.05
6	Thyme, seed	12"	.10
ANNUAL			
7	Chives, 1 plant		.10
8	Small fruited tomatoes, 12 plants or seeds (.15) . . .	1½'	.50
9	Peppers, 12 plants	1½"	.30
10	Scarlet Runner beans, seeds .	12"	.05
11	Parsley, seeds (biennial) . .	3"–6"	.05
12	Radish, seed	1"–2"	.05
13	Carrots, seeds	2"–3"	.10
14	New Zealand spinach, seed .	8"	.10
15	Calendulas, pot marigolds, seed	8"	.10
			$2.85

FIG. 6-7
"The Useful Border," *The Garden Magazine*,
April 1918

vegetable garden. Perennial vegetables and herbs—rhubarb, asparagus, horseradish, peppermint, sage, and thyme—are planted at the ends of the garden where they can remain unmolested when the annuals are planted. 'Scarlet Runner Beans' and tomatoes are trained along a back fence and provide splashes of color. Pepper plants or beets fill the middle of one half balanced by bright calendula (pot marigold) on the other, all framed by the gray greens of the sage and New Zealand spinach. Finally, feathery carrots and parsley provide the front border of the bed. Because she was selective in her choice of vegetables to achieve her desired effect, Strang admitted that this bed could not take the place of a regular vegetable garden. Nevertheless, she was correct in asserting that it would make an interesting supplement.

WAR GARDEN TO VICTORY GARDEN

At the eleventh hour of the eleventh day of the eleventh month in 1918, the guns fell silent and the war garden was decommissioned. The National War Garden Commission reissued its posters and booklets with the new title of *War Garden Victorious*. In 1919, Charles Pack published a book with the same title and argued that people should continue to plant vegetable gardens in order to ease the food shortage in postwar Europe.[11] The preface to the victory edition of the War Garden pamphlet states:

The war gardener's responsibility, therefore, did not end with the coming of peace. His War Garden must now be made a Victory Garden in the full sense of the words. It must help solve the problem of feeding people rendered helpless by years of ruthless and terrible war.[12]

Pack firmly believed that the home food gardening movement would continue. War gardens had shown people that they could lower their cost of living, grow and serve better quality food, and enjoy an inexpensive form of recreation. However, the

"Roaring Twenties" and advances in transportation and food preservation technologies once again relegated vegetable gardens to the background of American horticulture.[13] Whatever musings about the ornamental qualities of vegetable gardens that had begun to germinate during World War I lay dormant until America's entry into World War II thrust vegetable gardens to the forefront of the national consciousness.

WORLD WAR II AND THE VICTORY GARDEN

Within two weeks of the bombing of Pearl Harbor in December 1941, Secretary of Agriculture Claude Wickard called a National Defense Gardening meeting in Washington, D. C. Oddly enough, the purpose was not to encourage war or defense gardens, but to develop a program to actively discourage inexperienced people from planting new vegetable gardens. Wickard had valid concerns. First, he did not believe there was a food shortage looming. Second, if extra food had to be produced, it was best left to professionals. Many fields lay idle that could be put into production by farmers. Novice gardeners were notoriously wasteful of seed, fertilizer, and pesticides. Third, he was concerned that a sense of panic might overtake the country. Many people remembered the food riots in New York and the famine fears that had gripped the nation after America joined the Great War. The official promotion of war gardens might raise that specter once

again. Finally, the Department of Agriculture was probably still smarting over having been outshone by Pack and his organization during World War I. The Department of Agriculture considered Pack a publicity hound who had created near panic in the country, with the result that people ripped up their petunias and planted potatoes when there was really no need. In this new war, the Department of Agriculture was determined to establish early control of the situation.[14]

One issue that Secretary Wickard had not considered was the importance people placed on contributing to the war effort. Growing vegetables was one of the first ideas that leaped to many people's minds. As early as October 1941, classes in defense gardening were being taught in Detroit.[15] In 1942, seed companies and nurserymen reported that they were swamped with calls from concerned citizens.[16] As public demand for war gardens grew, Wickard was powerless to stop it, though he did try. He placed notices in horticultural magazines in the early months of 1942, urging garden clubs and community leaders to act as calming influences "to prevent hysteria" and to discourage "wholesale vegetable production" unless advised to do so by the proper authorities.[17] In January 1942, the Garden Club of America (GCA) announced that it was combining efforts with the Office of Civilian Defense to promote "a nation-wide increase in home and community truck gardens." By March 1942, news of victory gardens were on everybody's lips. The GCA had determined that their war project would be called "Victory Gardens" or "Home Food Supply,"

War Gardens Victorious

Copyright, 1919, National War Garden Commission.

Every War Garden a Peace Plant—
— Charles Lathrop Pack, President.

NATIONAL WAR GARDEN COMMISSION
WASHINGTON, D.C.
A POSTER FOR 1919, SYMBOLIC OF VICTORY

FIG. 6-8
This poster was part of Pack's attempts to continue the vegetable gardening movement after World War I. The version printed during the war showed a child and vegetables scrambling out of a trench. Here, they are marching home in victory. Despite the skill of Maginel Wright Enright Barney (1881–1966), a well-known illustrator of children's books and Frank Lloyd Wright's sister, the allure of new modern conveniences was too much, and Pack's postwar programs foundered. Reprinted from *The War Garden Victorious*, Charles Lathrop Pack

FIG. 6-9

FIG. 6-9
Spring in Town (1941), the last painting by
Grant Wood (1892–1942), was completed on the
eve of World War II. It captures an idealized view
of simple Midwestern life, including a vegetable
garden whose flower border has sprung to life.
The *Saturday Evening Post* put *Spring in Town*
on its April 18, 1942, cover. The painting encapsulated the American way of life that was being
defended, and reflected the growing popularity
of victory gardens as well.
Collection of The Sheldon Swope Art Museum,
Terre Haute, Indiana, © Estate of Grant
Wood/Licensed by VAGA, New York, NY

FIG. 6-9
Spring in Town (1941), the last painting by
Grant Wood (1892–1942), was completed on the
eve of World War II. It captures an idealized view
of simple Midwestern life, including a vegetable
garden whose flower border has sprung to life.
The *Saturday Evening Post* put *Spring in Town*
on its April 18, 1942, cover. The painting encapsulated the American way of life that was being
defended, and reflected the growing popularity
of victory gardens as well.
Collection of The Sheldon Swope Art Museum,
Terre Haute, Indiana, © Estate of Grant
Wood/Licensed by VAGA, New York, NY

FIG. 6-10
The federal government was initially reluctant
to promote vegetable gardening during World
War II. By 1943, however, the Secretary of
Agriculture had recognized that people needed
victory gardens, and the government issued
posters to promote the program. Aside from the
initial admonition not to plow under flowers, for
the most part government propaganda had little
to say about the appearance of victory gardens.
National Archives and Records Administration

and a "Garden for Victory" logo made its first appearance. Various horticulture magazines produced plans and planting schemes for first-time growers.[18] The Macmillan Company Press released six books on the topic of vegetable or victory gardens. Many 1942 seed catalogs included messages about planting a war, defense, or victory garden. The Doggett-Pfeil Company of Springfield, New Jersey, even advertised a Victory Garden Kit with matching patriotic labeling on packages of seeds, fertilizer, and pesticides—everything the first-time grower needed to get started.[19] When food rationing began in 1943, there would be no stopping victory gardens.[20]

Many parallels existed between the war gardens of World War I and the victory gardens of World War II. Once again, transportation facilities were dedicated to the war effort, making haulage of fresh foods and seeds from the fields to towns difficult. With the draft in effect, labor shortages began to affect all segments of the agriculture industry. Moreover, a significant portion of the labor force of West Coast truck farms had been Japanese Americans who were interned throughout the war (see "Victory Gardens in the Japanese American Internment Camps"). Fertilizer was also in short supply since nitrates were reserved for munitions production. A special Victory Garden 3-8-7 fertilizer was authorized for food production only.[21] Nevertheless, victory gardens cropped up in the nooks and crannies of America. Across the country, abandoned lots, schoolyards, and backyards were once again put into production. In New York City,

Rockefeller Plaza was planted with tomatoes, while beans often framed the skyline views from penthouses.[22] People grew what they wanted in the space that was available to them. While beginners were discouraged from planting temperamental vegetables that required a great deal of space, tomatoes, carrots, corn, lettuce, and cabbage flourished in many victory gardens—eighteen million of them in 1942 and twenty million the following year.[23] This huge demand, combined with bad weather conditions in 1941 and 1942, caused some vegetable varieties to be sold out completely. On March 21, 1943, the W. Atlee Burpee Company printed in the *New York Times* an apology for seed shortages and delays in filling orders.

Yet even with all these difficulties, most people endured their victory garden trials with a self-deprecating sense of humor. An anonymous columnist, known only as S.A.V.E. (a take-off on W.A.V.E.), wrote a series of articles for the *Garden Club of America Bulletin* in which she confessed her loathing for vegetables and her belief that the "attractive young man with the delectable samples from the California Fruit Company will not call at my door next summer."[24] However, she was resolute in her determination to continue and laid out the requirements for becoming a S.A.V.E.:

Take in grandchildren, legitimate or borrowed, without a nurse, thus releasing two younger women for harder work; that you slave in your own garden, and that you have a consuming passion for canning. . . . Anyone taking in as many as three grandchildren automatically and just naturally becomes a Sergeant, and she who also puts

FIG. 6-11
Utility garden created by members of the
Northwest Section of the Garden Club of
America, New York, 1942
At the Twenty-ninth International Flower Show
held in New York City in April 1942, the section
devoted to "utility" gardens raised much interest. While not victory gardens per se, these
demonstration exhibits consciously attempted to
combine beauty and utility.
Smithsonian Institution, Archives of American
Gardens, Garden Club of America Collection,
photo: F. W. Cassebeer

up a thousand jars in 1943 can name her own rank.[25]
Chef June Platt, after noting that her maid did most
of the work in the victory garden while she tended the
roses and lawn, recounted her struggles with produce:
The Swiss chard was spectacular and I hate it. Two
packages for twenty cents and we ate and ate and
canned and canned and the garden is still full of it. I
served it to innocent guests and husband twenty-two
times, put up seven quarts of stems, and four quarts of
leaves, and hope to give away the rest of it.... And now
for the grand finale. I'm here to relate that two ten cent
packages of squash seed, planted in four hills at one end
of the garden eventually spread themselves over white
turnips, yellow turnips, green peppers and red peppers,
and were about to strangle the lima beans, when I inter-
fered and cut off the greedy runners.[26]

Ogden Nash in his own inimitable fashion
encapsulated his victory garden travails in a poem
published in *House and Garden Magazine* (see "My
Victory Garden").[27] Such writings served to reassure
readers that their efforts were not wasted, even if their
gardens did not look like the ones on the posters.

BEAUTIFYING THE VICTORY GARDEN

During World War II, there was an explicit appeal to
maintain the beauty of gardens, both vegetable and
ornamental. As had been the case with the war gardens of World War I, people began to look for ways
to make their vegetable gardens more attractive.
The obvious approach was to combine flowers and
vegetables in a garden. However, just as some vegetable seeds were in short supply, such was also the
case with flowers. Between seventy-five and ninety
percent of the acreage formerly devoted to growing
flowers in America was switched over to vegetable
production during the war.[28]

Seedsmen and nurseries marketed the flowers
that were available to victory gardeners. They
offered patriotic flowers—red, white, and blue combinations of every sort—to beautify the garden.
Each seed company thought its flowers were the
perfect companions for vegetables in a victory garden. The Dahliadel firm promoted dahlias, while
Pitzonka's Pansy Farm encouraged pansies for the
victory garden. Flowers were also given patriotic
names. General Douglas MacArthur's namesakes
included a rose, daffodil, snapdragon, gladiolus, and
dahlia. There were the 'Pearl Harbor Memory' rose,

MY VICTORY GARDEN OGDEN NASH

Today, my friends, I beg your pardon,
But I'd like to speak of my Victory Garden.
With a hoe for a sword, and citronella for armor,
I ventured forth to become a farmer.
On bended knee, and perspiring clammily,
I pecked at the soil to feed my family,
A figure than which there was none more dramatic-er.
Alone with the bugs, and my faithful sciatica.
I toiled with the patience of Job or Buddha,
But nothing turned out the way it shudda.

Would you like a description of my parsley?
I can give it to you in one word—gharsley!
They're making playshoes out of my celery,
It's reclaimed rubber, and purplish yellery,
Something crawly got into my chives,
My lettuce has hookworm, my cabbage has hives,
And I mixed the labels when sowing my carrots;
I planted birdseed—it came up parrots.
Do you wonder then, that my arteries harden
Whenever I think of my Victory Garden?

My farming will never make me famous,
I'm an agricultural ignoramus,
So don't ask me to tell a string bean from a soy bean.
I can't even tell a girl bean from a boy bean.

FIG. 6-12
Farm Security Administration Trailer Camp, Arlington, Virginia, April 1942. One of the most striking features of the victory garden movement was how quickly it spread. Without a concentrated educational or advertising campaign by the federal government, victory gardens began to appear all over the country in 1942. The lack of a centralized archive creates difficulties for historians studying victory gardens because the story is scattered throughout local garden club records, small town newspapers, and the memories of aging victory gardeners. Local control resulted in victory gardens that were wonderfully individualistic. Gardeners were free to express their creativity—this gentleman painted his fence red, white, and blue and posted a victory sign. The Library of Congress

the 'Mme. Chiang Kai-shek' mum, and the 'Stalin' and 'Jeep' dahlias. The most direct approach, though, was to give free flower seeds with the purchase of a vegetable garden assortment. Condon's Seed Company included sweet peas and nasturtiums in its vegetable collections. Burpee offered yellow and orange cosmos, 'Victory Marigolds,' giant zinnias, and red, white, and blue cornflowers with its vegetable assortments. A common practice was to plant the flowers along the edges of the vegetable garden, as a "Snip and Sniff" border.[29]

Instead of planting flowers in the vegetable garden, some gardeners planted vegetables in the flower garden. This idea was popular in early 1942 for people who did not have time to prepare separate vegetable gardens. In *Gardens for Victory*, Jean-Marie Putnam suggested asparagus, rhubarb, and Jerusalem artichoke as companions for perennial

beds, and carrots, beets, parsnips, and turnips in place of the usual flowering bulbs.[30] *House Beautiful* magazine suggested direct substitutions of vegetables for annual flowers to fill in around perennials (see table 1).[31]

Gardeners also began to think more sympathetically about the aesthetics of the vegetable garden. Some suggested making gardens more formal, and the idea of drift plantings in the vegetable garden was also revisited.[32] One victory garden beautification program was undertaken by J. Horace McFarland at his Breeze Hill farm. McFarland (1859–1948) was a leading figure in American horticulture. He is especially well known for his work with roses and served as the president of the American Rose Society. In 1889, he established Mount Pleasant Press and began his career as a printer of horticulture magazines, books, and seed catalogs.

In 1909, McFarland bought Breeze Hill farm, nearly two and one-half acres outside Harrisburg, Pennsylvania, where he lived and planted test gardens. By 1942, he had representative specimens of more than 1,164 plant species planted at Breeze Hill, including at least 888 varieties of roses. His Mount Pleasant Press owned a collection of more than fifty thousand images of plants, many of them taken at the farm. Breeze Hill was open to the public several days a week, and McFarland published a guidebook to his gardens for his visitors. In an occasional newsletter, *Breeze Hill News*, and in his numerous horticultural columns, he discussed the latest horticultural offerings and how they fared at Breeze Hill.[33]

The vegetable garden at Breeze Hill had a typical history. In the 1924 guidebook, three vegetable gardens are shown on the map. In 1927, the three had been reduced to one and by 1940, no vegetable garden is shown at all. In 1942, McFarland planted a victory garden at Breeze Hill. While he wrote of enjoying its fresh produce, like the rest of the gardens at Breeze Hill, his victory garden was really for show. In addition to educating his visitors, McFarland needed to generate photographs for his clients to use in their catalogs. Therefore, his victory garden was small, only thirty-five feet square, and surrounded by a white picket fence, "to make it look as much as possible like a small home garden."[34] To be marketable, it also had to be pleasing in appearance. As McFarland noted:

Many visitors to our Victory garden have been surprised at the beauty of it. Feathery carrot tops, curly parsley,

healthy red cabbage, and colorful peppers combine to rival any flower-bed you ever saw! There's no reason why vegetables beds can't have borders just as other plantings have. Here is where vegetables and flowers can be combined: beets, for example, make a fine border for a flower-bed. We reversed the idea, and used sweet alyssum to edge our vegetable garden.[35]

Throughout the war years, McFarland's victory garden expanded well beyond its white picket fence, though it continued to provide inspiration to visitors and advertising imagery for his customers. At the same time that some Americans sought

(OPPOSITE) FIG. 6-13
Growing vegetable gardens during wartime was not a phenomenon limited to America. Both the Allied and Axis powers encouraged their citizens to plant gardens. Despite the imminent danger of the Blitz, Londoners created beautiful as well as productive gardens. These Londoners added flowers to beautify a vegetable garden planted in a bomb crater.
Franklin D. Roosevelt Library

FIG. 6-14
This seed catalog, published by J. Horace McFarland and his Mount Pleasant Press, features the victory garden at Breeze Hill. The colorful tomatoes trained along the fence, the edging flowers, and ripe, abundant produce must have tempted more than one novice to take up gardening. Luckily, Ogden Nash was available for commiseration if the garden did not quite match the picture.
Smithsonian Institution Libraries, Horticulture Branch Library

FIG. 6-15
This undated image is probably from the early history of McFarland's Breeze Hill before ornamentals had "chased out" the vegetables in the 1930s.
Smithsonian Institution, Archives of American Gardens, J. Horace McFarland Collection

ways to beautify the mundane appearance of their victory gardens, another group used victory gardens to beautify desolate landscapes of suspicion and imprisonment.

VICTORY GARDENS IN THE JAPANESE AMERICAN INTERNMENT CAMPS

We are at war with Japan, and yet we have American citizens, born and brought up in this country, whose parents are Japanese. This is the essential problem.

Eleanor Roosevelt, *Collier's* magazine, 1943

Eleanor Roosevelt spoke no more than the simple truth in the opening lines of her essay. The attack on Pearl Harbor frightened Americans. Within days of the attack, paranoia and racism combined to produce a widespread hysteria that branded Japanese Americans as possible spies and saboteurs.[36] The government responded by forcibly removing more than one hundred thousand Japanese Americans living on the west coast and incarcerating them in hastily constructed camps, euphemistically termed "relocation centers." During the years spent in these camps, the position of Japanese Americans was truly untenable. Could they remain loyal to a country that had stripped them of their rights and presumed them to be enemies? A very few rejected the country that had rejected them; more decided to ride out the storm. While interned, many young Japanese American men enlisted in the U.S. armed

FIG. 6-16
Another commercial image taken by McFarland of his victory garden, July 11, 1942, I believe is his most charming.
Smithsonian Institution, Archives of American Gardens, J. Horace McFarland Collection

forces, forming the most decorated army regiment in American military history. For those who remained in the camps, planting victory gardens was another signal that they kept faith with American ideals despite the injustice done to them.[37] Just as important though, the gardens within the camps were a connection to the prewar life of the internees; they could, if not beautify, at least mitigate the harsh landscape behind the barbed wire.

Before the war, about half of the Japanese Americans living in California were employed in farming or marketing vegetables. Because Japanese immigrants were prohibited from owning land, they often specialized in crops that required intensive care and could be grown profitably on small plots. By one estimate, Japanese American farmers produced over ninety percent of the snap beans, strawberries, and celery, and approximately half of the artichokes, cauliflower, cucumbers, and tomatoes in California. Other members of the Japanese American community grew fruits and flowers or worked as professional landscapers and gardeners; however, the cultivation of vegetables was the economic underpinning of their communities.[38]

FIG. 6-17
Momoyo Yamamoto, formerly of Fresno, California, shown here topping a Daikon, a large radishlike vegetable which is a great delicacy among the Japanese people. It is eaten raw, cooked, or pickled. The seed for this crop was loaned by Min Omata, unit foreman, from Fresno, California. This center harvested 65 acres of this vegetable, and was the only WRA project growing it in large quantities.
WRA Photo no. D-659, photo: Francis Stewart, Rivers, Arizona, 11/25/42

FIG. 6-18
One of the many small victory gardens seen throughout the Rohwer Center.
WRA Photo no. H-495, photo: Charles E. Mace, McGehee, Arkansas, 6/16/44

FIG. 6-19
Closing of the Jerome Center, Denson, Arkansas.
The decorative flower garden at the approach to the center's administrative buildings was tended up to the last days by any flower lover who still remained in the center. Its fate after [the] final closing date was uncertain.
WRA Photo No. H-458, photo: Charles E. Mace, Denson, Arkansas, 6/23/44

On February 19, 1942, President Franklin D. Roosevelt signed Executive Order No. 9066, defining exclusion zones along the west coast and empowering the military to remove people of Japanese ancestry from those areas. Over the next few months, military authorities rounded up more than 113,000 Japanese Americans. Two-thirds of the detainees were citizens by birth. More than 17,000 children under the age of ten and 2,000 men and women over the age of sixty-five were among those taken to processing centers and shipped to ten camps in six states. Each camp eventually would hold between 7,000 and 19,000 internees.[39]

Surviving photographs of the camps provide only a dim reflection of the desolate scene that confronted the internees after their departure from the verdant landscapes of the west coast.[40] Some camps were located in swamps and others in deserts. All were isolated. Internees in northern camps faced winter temperatures of 30 degrees below zero while living in poorly insulated buildings. In southern camps, temperatures soared to above 100 degrees in the summer. Gusting wind and driving rain produced blinding dust storms or muddy morasses. Internees suffered from malaria, valley fever, dysentery, typhus, polio, and salmonella poisoning. Potable water was often in short supply; however, the small quantity and poor quality of food from government rations produced the most serious chronic health problems in all the camps.[41]

Government plans called for the camps to be as self-sufficient as possible. Hundreds of acres surrounding each camp were set aside for internees to cultivate vegetables and other crops, including daikon, a variety of radish much prized by the Japanese. In addition to working in the fields, though, many internees grew smaller vegetable gardens near their barracks. As victory garden terminology came into common usage during the war, many internees embraced it to describe their own vegetable gardens.[42] Like the long lines of young men and women volunteering for military service, victory gardens were a visible sign that the internees were "doing their bit" on the home front. The War Relocation Authority, the government agency in charge of the internees, took hundreds of photographs of the camps and the resettled families. Victory gardens were a common, highly visible component of these carefully staged compositions. In addition to supplementing inadequate food supplies and demonstrating patriotism, there was another motivation behind the creation of vegetable gardens.

To facilitate the erection of barracks, barbed wire fences, and guard posts, all native vegetation at the campsites had been cleared by bulldozers. The sterilized landscapes of the camps deeply disturbed the arriving internees, many of whom had made their living growing plants. Some were reduced to tears upon their arrival.[43] Minoru Yasui described her initial impression of the Minidoka camp near Twin Falls, Idaho: "No trees or anything green—only scrubby sagebrush and an occasional low cactus, and mostly dry, baked earth."[44] As internees tried to adjust to life behind barbed wire, planting seeds seemed a natural first step.[45] A camp

FIG. 6-20
Granada Relocation Center, Amache, Colorado. Fourth grade girl—Diane Wallace—weeding the school victory garden.
WRA Photo no. B-604, photo: Joe McClelland, Amache, Colorado, 6/4/43

newsletter stated it plainly: "[We must apply] our combined energies to the grim task of conquering the elements and converting a wasteland into an inhabitable community."[46] The internees pooled their horticultural expertise. Some had brought seeds from their homes to the camps. Others evaluated soil conditions and devised irrigation schemes.[47] Miné Okubo, in her memoir of camp life at Topaz in Utah, described the bucket brigades for plant watering that formed each evening between the laundry buildings and the gardens.[48] With unrelenting effort, the internees remade the camps. "Gardens had sprung up everywhere, in the firebreaks, between the rows of barracks—rock gardens, vegetable gardens, cactus and flower gardens" is how Jeanne Wakatsuki Houston described the transformation at Manzanar in California.[49]

Some of the horticultural creations were truly spectacular. Professional landscape architects and gardeners among the internees crafted entire miniature landscapes with ponds, cascades, and intricate rock formations. The care taken is clearly seen in figure 6-19, where only the guard tower in the background mars the delicate line of the planting design. Even at the temporary assembly centers, internees had planted gardens, knowing they might be gone when the plants came to fruition. As she departed from the Fresno assembly center for an internment camp, Mary Tsukamoto noted the fruits of their labor: "So many beautiful flowers and vegetables, so lush and green. . . . Who but *Nihonjins* (Japanese) would leave a place like that in beauty?"[50]

THE AFTERMATH

After World War II, there were no more victory gardens. Some activists lobbied for the continuation of community garden programs, but only a few urban allotment programs continued. To some degree, this was a pragmatic response to the new reality posed by the Cold War. A vegetable garden would be of little use in a nuclear war. Throughout the 1950s and 1960s, patios, manicured lawns, and neat flower beds were the dominant image of postwar suburban America. Vegetable gardens slowly faded from popular consciousness. From *I Love Lucy* to *The Brady Bunch*, from the Cosbys to the Osbournes, one is hard-pressed to find a vegetable garden represented on American television.

7

THE GLORIOUS
VEGETABLE GARDEN

In a flash, I saw how beautiful vegetables could be.

Rebecca Gray, "Redesigning the Kitchen Garden,"
Garden Design Magazine, February/March 1996

*I don't have a vegetable garden. I have a garden
and vegetables grow in it.*

Robert Dash, artist and owner of Madoo Gardens, c. 1983

In the mid-1970s, spiraling inflation sparked renewed interest in vegetable gardens. People realized that even small gardens could make a significant dent in their cost of living. The baby boomers cultivating these gardens modeled them on the victory gardens of their childhood: utilitarian gardens characterized by straight rows and traditional vegetables. Over the next decade, food prices decreased, but a burgeoning population of yuppies continued to garden. Moreover, they began to remake the traditional vegetable garden.[1]

Though not the first, the most influential work for this new generation of vegetable gardeners was Rosalind Creasy's *The Complete Book of Edible Landscaping.* Creasy spoke to the more sophisticated environmental awareness that was born during the 1960s. She showed how to create gardens that were more environmentally friendly than "water-hungry hydrangeas and fertilizer-hungry floriferous fuchsias."[2] However, beauty did not have to be sacrificed for bounty. Creasy carefully delineated how vegetables and other food plants could be used to create aesthetically pleasing landscapes. Though she preferred informal, natural gardens, Creasy recognized that edibles could be planted in more elaborate, formal arrangements. Specifically, she reminded her readers of the ornamental vegetable gardens of the seventeenth and eighteenth centuries that were laid out in parterres and edged with box hedge. With her new approach to "foodscaping," vegetables could appear anywhere in the landscape; locations were limited only by the gardener's imagination. Simply put, her work erased the line between the vegetable garden and the ornamental garden.[3]

With Creasy's hugely popular book in hand, yuppies took to vegetable gardening with a vengeance.[4] By June 1988, *Time* magazine proclaimed: "America returns to the Garden."[5] From that time until today, books and magazine articles have celebrated the new vegetable garden in all its diversity, though certain themes are often echoed. First, new economic realities mean that people have less time to work in their gardens and less space to grow them in. Gardens are now smaller and planted more thickly to cut down on weeding.[6] Community gardens well illustrate this phenomenon. The development of miniature varieties means that one could plant all one's vegetables on a patio, in flower baskets, or on a balcony.[7] Second, with smaller gardens there is less emphasis on a large summer harvest to be canned or frozen for winter use. Instead, the vegetable garden is used to produce fresh food for as long as the growing season allows.[8] Third, more people are willing to share their gardens with wildlife, and some have abandoned fences altogether.[9] Fourth, the popularity of new ethnic cuisines means gardeners actively seek out exotic vegetables.[10] Finally, historical inspiration has played a significant role in popularizing the growing of vegetables. Visitors to the restored gardens of Château Villandry, Colonial Williamsburg, the William Paca House and Garden, Monticello, and Mount Vernon now have an opportunity to admire the heirloom vegetable varieties grown at these sites.[11]

All these factors have shaped the appearance of the "new" vegetable garden. At the most basic, appearance is important because smaller lots and less time mean vegetable gardens are nearer to houses and are far more visible than ever before. This compression also means gardeners are more likely to blend vegetable and flower gardens. Moving from simply edging their vegetable gardens with flowers to intermixing the two freely, people expect their gardens to do double duty—provide both food and a pleasing landscape. Smaller gardens make it more practical to plant in beds, which inspire people to try more unusual combinations than are traditionally found in gardens of orderly rows.

The layout of vegetable gardens has become outrageously individualistic. At one end of the spectrum are formal designs that are planted with vegetables instead of flowers. Landscape architects, whose professional ancestors scorned the kitchen garden, are called upon to design vegetable gardens.[12] Geometric parterres planted with vegetables and edged with box have become a common sight. Neat groupings of lettuce and tomatoes form artistic counterpoints to showy dahlias, tulips, and roses. Quintinie would likely enjoy a stroll through many a modern American vegetable garden.[13] However, no style is out of bounds. Elizabethan-knot gardens and Italianate-inspired piazzas also sprout vegetables.[14]

At the other extreme are the naturalistic examples. Strolling through these gardens is like walking through a meadow of wild vegetables. Vegetables seem to be left to their own devices. Asparagus and carrots produce long feathery foliage, while chives send up purple balls of flowers and colorful beans cascade down poles.

Regardless of the layout, people are spending much more time contemplating the colors and textures of their vegetable gardens.[15] The architecture of beds and rows is carefully planned so that colors flow and complement each other.[16] Differences in height, contrasting textures, and myriad shades of green provide visual interest as the vegetables mature.[17] Detailed guides that chronicle the ornamental characteristics of hundreds of vegetable varieties are now widely available. Varieties are as likely to be recommended for their early flowers or interesting foliage as for their final produce. Gardeners now think of vegetables in exactly the same way they used to think of flowers.[18]

Photographs of vegetable gardens from the Archives of American Gardens illustrate many of the themes discussed above. The diversity in size and form is striking. Some vegetable gardens are composed of a few rows of tomatoes and cabbages. Others are complex menageries of exotic plants. A common feature is the owners' pride in the beauty of their vegetable gardens.

FIG. 7-2
The Madoo Conservancy, Sagaponack,
New York, 1995
Long before baby boomers and their disposable incomes fueled the craze for designer vegetable gardens, the artist Robert Dash created his gardens at Madoo. Since 1967, Dash has brought a painter's eye to his gardens, which he treats like a canvas. Using a basic layout of a circle divided into wedges, Dash continually alters his vegetables, questing after the perfect visual composition. He has gone so far as to repaint the garden furniture to match whatever is in bloom.
Photo: Robert Dash

FIG. 7-3
Whisler Garden, Carmel, California, 1996
At the Whisler home in California, the vegetable garden has been brought right onto the patio of the house. Planter boxes of different sizes encourage an ever-changing mixture of flowers, herbs, and vegetables.
Smithsonian Institution, Archives of American Gardens, Garden Club of America Collection, photo: Mary R. Whisler

FIG. 7-4
The Matthews Garden, Paradise Valley, Arizona, 1992
This garden is situated on the side of a hill in the Sonoran desert. The vegetable garden is one of a series of "pocket" gardens and patios framed by native stone. The nooks and crannies provide a perfect stage in which to intermingle vegetables, ornamentals, and the occasional scarecrow.
Smithsonian Institution, Archives of American Gardens, Garden Club of America Collection, photo: Pam Singleton

FIG. 7-5
Post Corners Apartment Homes, Centerville, Virginia, 1996
In the 1990s, the Post Company discovered that residents at its properties, located throughout the southern United States, wanted to garden. At several of its locations, the company set aside areas for gardens. The raised beds filled with flowers and vegetables not only encourage a feeling of community but also brighten the view from residents' windows.
Smithsonian Institution, Archives of American Gardens, Garden Club of America Collection, photo: Todd T. Tibbitts

FIG. 7-6
Entrance to the community vegetable garden, Post Brookhaven Apartment Homes, Atlanta, Georgia, 1997
Smithsonian Institution, Archives of American Gardens, Garden Club of America Collection, photo: Todd T. Tibbitts

FIG. 7-7
The Brooklyn Botanic Garden has a long history
of community gardening. These photographs,
separated by sixty years, show the ongoing appeal
of allotment gardening especially for children.
Children's Garden at the Brooklyn Botanic
Garden, New York, 1982, photo: Tom Twente

FIG. 7-8
Children's Garden at the Brooklyn Botanic
Garden, 1924
Courtesy Brooklyn Botanic Garden, photo: Louis
Buhle, Brooklyn Botanic Garden staff photographer

(OPPOSITE) FIG. 7-9
Rev. Willie Jennings tending the vegetables
in the Sugar Hill Community Education Garden,
Houston, Texas, mid-1990s
Part of the Urban Harvest program, this garden
was created to show residents of Houston's econom-
ically deprived Third Ward what could be grown on
a very small piece of land. City buses made regular
stops for passengers to view the garden.
Smithsonian Institution, Archives of American
Gardens, photo: George M. McAfee Jr.

FIG. 7-10

Blue Briar Cottage and Garden, Asheville, North Carolina, 1996

When the owners of Blue Briar Cottage were designing their garden, they wished to be able to stroll along the mountainside. In keeping with this open theme, the vegetable garden is not fenced off and can be viewed from the gazebo that overlooks the pleasure garden.

Smithsonian Institution, Archives of American Gardens, Garden Club of America Collection, photo: Carolyn A. Humphries

FIG. 7-11
The Rain Dragon Garden, 2001
Northwest Flower and Garden Show,
Seattle, Washington
According to its creator, Cindy Morrison,
not only the inspiration but also the material
for this award-winning garden came from a
trip to China. While traveling among
remote villages near the Laos border,
Morrison purchased seeds from local markets, having been attracted by the colorful
packets. Returning to her home in
Washington, she planted the seeds and used
the ensuing vegetables to craft a beautiful,
intimate vegetable garden. Though strongly
influenced by the gardens of the Chinese
villagers she met on her trip, Morrison
enlivened her garden with topiary elephants
and a dragon (not visible). While topiary
design is her profession, at her home on
Vashon Island, she has spent the last twenty
years landscaping with edible plants.
Photo: David McDonald

FIG. 7-12
Boscobel Restoration, Garrison, New York, 1980s

FIG. 7-13
Cloches, like these at the vegetable gardens of
the William Paca House and Garden, have begun
to reappear in modern gardens. The glass jars are
effective for forcing early plants and add a decorative effect to many vegetable gardens.
Courtesy of The Historic Annapolis Foundation

(OPPOSITE) FIG. 7-14
Stony Brook, Princeton, New Jersey, 1995
Colorful flowers and white split-rail fences
frame this beautiful vegetable garden.
Smithsonian Institution, Archives of American
Gardens, Garden Club of America Collection,
photo: Diane B. Clarke

FIG. 7-15
Wister Garden, Oldwick, New Jersey, 1980s
This historically inspired vegetable garden is an ideal companion to the eighteenth-century house against which it is nestled. Here the vegetables take center stage, while flowers form color borders. The dense plantings fill in the geometry of the layout and lessen the amount of time spent weeding.
Smithsonian Institution, Archives of American Gardens,
Garden Club of America Collection, photo: Molly Adams

FIG. 7-16
Wick Farm, Morristown, New Jersey, c. 1986
The restored vegetable garden at Wick Farm helps to complete the scene for visitors to this historic site.
Smithsonian Institution, Archives of American Gardens,
Garden Club of America Collection, photo: Molly Adams

FIG. 7-17
Community Gardens at Edgerton Park,
New Haven, Connecticut, 2000
In 1965, philanthropist Frederick
Brewster donated his estate to the
city of New Haven for a park. In the
1980s, the site of the original kitchen
garden was transformed into community gardens. Now many miniature
vegetable gardens flourish where
there once was only one.
Smithsonian Institution, Archives
of American Gardens, Garden Club
of America Collection, photo:
Jennifer Radford

FIG. 7-18
Coke Garden, Dallas, Texas, 1996
Here is another example of a formal
approach to the vegetable garden.
Landscape designer Carl Neels
planned a series of simplified parterres
that radiate from the central statue.
While the vegetables provide more
height than classic parterres, the box
edging supplies crisp definitions that
hearken back to the earliest French
gardens.
Smithsonian Institution, Archives of
American Gardens, Garden Club of
America Collection, photo: Caroline
L. Hunt

FIG. 7-19
Buttonbrook, Far Hills, New Jersey, c. 1967
Boxwood edging adds a formal touch to an
otherwise rustic garden.
Smithsonian Institution, Archives of
American Gardens, Garden Club of America
Collection

FIG. 7-20
Mulberry House, Potomac, Maryland, 2001
A statue of St. Francis of Assisi is a delightful
ornament in this garden filled with exotics.
Smithsonian Institution, Archives of
American Gardens, Garden Club of America
Collection, photo: Sarah Hood Salomon

(OPPOSITE) FIG. 7-21
Community Gardens at Edgerton Park, New Haven,
Connecticut, 2000
Smithsonian Institution, Archives of American Gardens,
Garden Club of America Collection, photo: Jennifer Radford

FIG. 7-22
Hidden Glen, Meadowbrook, Pennsylvania, 1998
Bee skeps and pyramidal vegetable trellises add visual interest to
this vegetable garden. In the 1980s, horticulturalist Charles Gale
reintegrated the vegetable garden with the rest of the gardens.
Smithsonian Institution, Archives of American Gardens,
Garden Club of America Collection, photo: Shelley D. Schorsch

FIG. 7-23
Purtell Garden, Milwaukee, Wisconsin, c. 1996
A typical modern gardener, Hattie Purtell wanted her vegetable garden to be a source of organic vegetables as well as a place where she could introduce her grandchildren to nature and the joys of gardening. With an eye toward color and composition in the individual plots, landscape architect Judith Stark designed this vegetable garden to complement the natural landscape effect of the rest of the garden. Smithsonian Institution, Archives of American Gardens, Garden Club of America Collection, photo: © Tony Casper

FIG. 7-24
Haskell Garden, New Bedford, Massachusetts, 2001
On the grounds of his nursery, award-winning horticulturist
Allen Haskell has created a beautiful set of display gardens,
which includes this vegetable garden. Gigantic cabbages and
squashes overhung by sunflowers must surely tempt both the
avocational and professional gardeners among his customers.
Smithsonian Institution, Archives of American Gardens,
Garden Club of America Collection, photo: John S. Penney Jr.

FIG. 7-25
This lovely vegetable garden in Mendham, New Jersey (1980s), was designed by Sieglinde Anderson of Hope, New Jersey.
Smithsonian Institution, Archives of American Gardens, Garden Club of America Collection, photo: Molly Adams

FIG. 7-26
Haskell Garden, New Bedford, Massachusetts, 2001
Smithsonian Institution, Archives of American Gardens, Garden Club of America Collection, photo: John S. Penney Jr.

FIG. 7-27
Longfield Garden, Prospect, Kentucky, 1995
In the 1990s, North Hill Associates was brought in to transform this vegetable garden. Plans included gravel walks and a pergola with grapevine. This "before" version of the vegetable garden already shows much ornamental appeal.
Smithsonian Institution, Archives of American Gardens, Garden Club of America Collection, photo: Edith S. Bingham

FIG. 7-28
Rehder Garden, Wilmington, North Carolina, 1997
While parterres and raised beds have opened new avenues for elaborating the vegetable garden, many people find a simple beauty in old-fashioned rows of vegetables. As this garden clearly shows, artful arrangements of color and textures are not limited to any particular style of vegetable garden.
Smithsonian Institution, Archives of American Gardens, Garden Club of America Collection, photo: Henry B. Rehder

FIG. 7-29
Valentine Garden, Santa Barbara, California, 1985
A small vegetable plot coexists with a rock-crop garden on this patio.
Smithsonian Institution, Archives of American Gardens, Garden Club of America Collection,
photo: Eleanor C. Weller

8

FEAST OR FANCY
The Ornamental Vegetable

Among modern gardening aficionados, the term "ornamental vegetable" usually encompasses four species—eggplant, sweetpotato, peppers, and cabbage or kale—that now have both edible and ornamental varieties. Over the last fifteen years or so, the use of all of these ornamental vegetables has increased for two reasons.[1] One, they fulfill practical horticultural necessities. Ornamental cabbage provides color in the fall, brightening as temperatures plummet. Ornamental peppers also bring color to the garden in early autumn or, if moved indoors, banish winter blues with vivid reds and yellows. Ornamental sweetpotato vine is a luscious groundcover that grows faster than kudzu. Yet even with all these pragmatic recommendations, the appeal of ornamental vegetables lies as much in their novelty as in the fact that they are vegetables. Like a painter, the sophisticated gardener sees a certain meatiness in ornamental vegetables that is lacking in their flimsy, floral counterparts. As twenty-first-century gardeners deliberately blur the line between the vegetable and flower garden, it is not surprising that they also seek to erase the distinction between flower and vegetable.

FIG. 8-1
Sake bottle in eggplant form
Japanese, Edo period, 19th century
Clay, 15.1 x 7.9 cm
Freer Gallery of Art, Smithsonian Institution,
Washington, D.C., Gift of Charles Lang Freer

The chic ornamental vegetable is not a purely postmodern, deconstuctionist, existential phenomenon. Indeed, ornamental vegetables in the Western gardening tradition have a much older history than most people realize, one that began with the Islamic expansion of the late Middle Ages. At that time the first exotic-looking, and seemingly inedible, vegetable was introduced to Europe—the eggplant. A few hundred years later, tomatoes and chilies arrived from the New World. Again apparently inedible, but admired and grown for their ornamental qualities. Nor was this a purely European phenomenon. In the 1700s, the Japanese chose to create an ornamental from the unpalatable European kale. So many ornamental vegetables and more prosaic ornamentals, for that matter, are simply exotic, unappetizing foods. However, by the early twentieth century, tomato, eggplant, and chilies were all commonly accepted as food by Europeans and Americans. For the most part, their former ornamental appeal had faded from the collective horticulture memory. So, how did modern ornamental vegetables come about?

Certainly, the proximal cause is the edible landscaping revolution of the 1980s. However, even before that, I think the seeds were first sown during the war and victory garden movements. During that time, people thought not only about the appearance of their vegetable gardens, but also about the possible aesthetic appeal of vegetables themselves.

In May 1917, an editorial in *The House Beautiful* magazine entitled "A Vegetable Year" starts with a simple question, central to this book: "We wonder why it is that when a thing becomes useful we are in danger of losing all sense of beauty in it." After recounting the former ornamental appeal of the tomato in its love-apple days (see "Love Those Love Apples"), the author continues:

And yet, like everything else, this is not a new thing. We know several persons who admire vegetables. One friend of ours utilizes Indian corn in his borders along with cannas, elephant ears, castor beans, and other tropical looking growths. Another friend plants a succession of lettuce in the same bed with his succession of poppies . . . you cannot tell where the flower ends and the vegetable begins.[2]

There is no evidence that vegetables became a popular motif, and the editorial has a definite tongue-in-cheek tone, suggesting, for example, that suitors present their lady loves with bouquets of vegetables. Nonetheless, the sentiment was continued in an editorial the following March, observing that people were approaching the seed catalogs with dreams of 1918's vegetable garden: "How we pour [sic] over the lineaments of a rutabaga, how our hearts expand before the Rubenesque contours of a cow-beet! We know just the kind of spines a well behaved cucumber has and how beautifully blond and buttery the head of a lady-like lettuce is."[3] One doubts that such flowery prose would have been expended on vegetables were it not for the fact that people were spending a lot of time thinking and talking about war gardens.

Early in the victory garden movement, various authors suggested planting vegetables in the flower garden. However, this was a remedy for a lack of space, not a belief that vegetables should be treated as ornamentals in their own right. Before the war, only a very few vegetables were considered to have any aesthetic appeal at all. Sweetpotato vine was occasionally grown indoors as a trailing houseplant. The author who wrote under the name S.A.V.E., in one of her confessions, notes that she planted cabbage for effect rather than consumption.[4] An article in the *Garden Club of America Bulletin* for May 1942 casually mentions ornamental kale as a low maintenance plant that could be planted in the garden to wait out the war.[5] As had been the case during World War I, gardeners began to reexamine the aesthetic qualities of other vegetables.

In victory garden harvest shows held around the country, prizes were awarded not only for the largest vegetables but also for the most artistic arrangement of vegetables or their flowers. In 1942, *The Flower Grower* magazine discussed the overlooked beauty of the flowers produced by sweet pepper, watermelon, bean, eggplant, and tomato.[6] Dried okra pods combined with Bells of Ireland and Devils's Claws were a suggestion for a striking floral arrangement, while 'White Velvet' or 'Creole' okra was recommended for the garden.[7] *Gardens for Victory* suggested shallow container plantings using beet, carrot, and Swiss chard for interior decoration, likening them to a living oil painting.[8] The new 'Rhubarb Chard' was noted by several authors as being a lovely addition to the victory garden, and not at all out of place in a rose garden.[9] The bronze-leaf 'Mignonette' and oak-leaf lettuces were considered the most attractive of the salad plants.[10]

As had been the case with vegetable gardens, interest in ornamental vegetables apparently waned in the postwar years. Tulips and roses supplanted the ornamental okra and 'Rhubarb Chard'. Yet, all the elements of the modern fascination with ornamental vegetables were present during the war years. Therefore, in the never-ending quest to find something new and unusual for the garden, it is only appropriate that we look back at the history of some of these ornamental vegetables.

THE ALWAYS ORNAMENTAL EGGPLANT
(SOLANUM MELONGENA L.)

A monstrosity left behind by a mutant Easter bunny is the only explanation for such a globular, purple vegetable being called an eggplant. It doesn't look like an egg. It doesn't taste like an egg. So where did the name come from? Well, like its distant relative the tomato, the eggplant was first introduced into the gardens of the English-speaking world as an ornamental. An early, white-skinned variety looked for all the world like eggs growing on a bush; hence its name in English. The gradual acceptance of eggplant as food has obscured its ornamental heritage, but adventurous gardeners have rediscovered not only the original "eggy" eggplant but also a whole slew of new and unusual forms that are enlivening the vegetable and flower garden.

Eggplant has an ancient history. It was first domesticated in India. A multitude of Sanskrit names and the many forms of the fruit point to its long cultivation in India. *Brinjal*, as eggplant is commonly known, forms a standard part of the Indian culinary repertoire. For example, it was the main dish served at a fifteenth-century royal feast, where the curried eggplant was mixed with shredded coconut, cardamom, a little citrus juice, and camphor![11] The eggplant is also a much prized and ancient food in the Far East. It may even have been domesticated independently in China. The *Qiminyaoshu*, a Chinese agricultural treatise from the fifth century C.E., mentions eggplant, but describes them as very small and thorny, more reminiscent of the wild variety.[12] In Japan, references to eggplants have been found on wooden documents dating to the Nara period (eighth century). These *mokkan*, as they are called, were the memo pads and shipping labels of their day. Tens of thousands of *mokkan* have been found near the residence of Prince Nagaya (684–729) in the town of Nara. They described the shipping of vegetables to the prince's compound from the surrounding countryside, and the preparations for grand feasts: sea urchin, abalone, wild boar, deer, radish, cucumber, and eggplant were all regal delicacies.[13] Beyond princely tables, eggplants were so popular that farmers could sell the abundant crop in exchange for "night soil" to use as fertilizer. "Eggplants for pee" was apparently a commonly heard call in Japanese towns as late as the nineteenth century.[14]

Muslims brought the eggplant to Europe. In the seventh and eighth centuries, Islam spread from the Arabian peninsula to encompass three continents. Within the empire, a shared language and emphasis on learning encouraged scholars to travel widely and to synthesize their findings in treatises. Botany was a particularly popular area of study. From India, Muslim agronomists brought to the Mediterranean watermelons, eggplants, spinach, artichokes, cotton, and *colocasia*, among many other crops. These were all tropical plants that required extended periods of heat to ripen, but in the Mediterranean, summer was traditionally a fallow time in the fields. With improvements in irrigation and fertilizing schemes, Muslims were able to devise a summer planting scheme, and the subsequent cultivation of eggplant and its sister crops flourished all around the Mediterranean. Eggplant became a popular ingredient in Islamic cookery. A thirteenth-century cookbook contained over eighteen recipes for the vegetable. A famous eggplant dish is known as *imam bayildi*, or "the imam fainted," though whether the imam passed out from hunger, the luscious smell, or the cost of the olive oil for preparing the dish, I have yet to determine. Muslims also appreciated the finer points of eggplants. They composed poems about eggplants and admired their ornamental qualities. For example, a small white variety graced the pleasure garden of a fourteenth-century Yemeni king.[15]

For many centuries, northern Europeans considered the eggplant only as an ornamental. Because eggplant was a member of the deadly nightshade family (*Solanaceae*), most people assumed that it was poisonous. John Gerard, a sixteenth-century English botanist and author of the famous *Herbal*, sounded the warning in 1596:

But I rather wish English men to content themselves

Melanzana fructu pallido.

with the meat and sauce of our own Country, than with
fruit and sauce eaten with such peril: for doubtless
these apples have a mischievous quality. . . . Therefore
it is better to esteem this plant and have him in the
Garden for your pleasure and the rareness thereof, than
for any virtue or good qualities yet known.[16]

The Spanish brought eggplant to the Caribbean and South America, where it flourished in the tropical heat. In North America, Southerners seem to have readily taken to the new plant. Thomas Jefferson probably encountered the eggplant during his ambassadorship to France. His earliest mention is from a letter to his Monticello neighbor, the Count de Rieux. While undated and fragmentary, it is probably from around 1796, and contains the following postscript: "I was so pleased with the egg-plants

brought by Peter, and his dressing them according to the directions you were so good as to give, that I must ask some seed, and advice to cultivate them."[17] Jefferson experimented with eggplant at least from 1809 onward, but he never seemed to have had much luck. Over the years, he continually asked nurseryman Bernard McMahon for replacement seeds. He did note that one could buy eggplant in the market of Washington, D.C., though only for a very short time in the early fall.

We know that Jefferson's near contemporaries, the Peales, grew eggplant in Pennsylvania at least during the 1820s, when James Peale painted them. Yet botanist Henry Phillips noted in 1820 that not much progress had been made in the culinary acceptance of eggplant, or "vegetable egg," as he called it: "In England, the eggplant is principally cultivated for its singular and curious appearance, few families even knowing that they are proper for aliment, excepting those who have resided on the Continent, or who have studied the natural history of plants."[18] He then included some recipes from a friend who lived in the West Indies, noting that it was a popular food in the islands. Opinions about the eggplant continued to be divided for many more years.

In 1878, a seed company in Montreal, Canada, offered seven varieties of eggplant for sale to the public, five of which were explicitly marketed as ornamentals. Twenty years after that, in 1891, an anonymous writer put a notice in the journal *Science* stating that eggplant "had received little systematic attention, either from gardeners or students." After discussing his experiments in cultivating eggplants

FIG. 8-2
In 1606, Prince Bishop Johann Konrad von Gemmingen (1593/95–1612) of Eichstätt, Germany, commissioned a Nuremberg apothecary, Basilius Besler, to make copper engravings of the ornamental plants growing in the recently renovated gardens of his palace. Included among the exotic flowers was the eggplant, which was not widely eaten in Germany, even though it had been in Europe for centuries by this time. In this version of Besler's engraving, the eggplants are the pearly white of the early ornamental variety, while in another version the eggplants are colored purple.
Reprinted with permission from *The Garden at Eichstätt*, Benedikt Taschen Verlag

in the northern United States, the author concludes with four recipes in the hopes of encouraging his readers to give eggplant a whirl.

With the successful development of the deep purple culinary varieties like 'Black Beauty' and 'New York Improved,' the eggplant gradually found acceptance on American tables.[19] The old vegetable egg forms were gradually forgotten. So successful was this transformation that the word "eggplant" is now synonymous with a particular shade of purple and has been enshrined by the ultimate arbitrator of shades, hues, and tints: the crayon. Artists have also been continually attracted to those large, smooth, glossy purple fruits. I would even hazard a guess that the purple eggplant is the most commonly portrayed vegetable in paintings.

In the last decade, eggplant has made a strong ornamental comeback. Hundreds of varieties are now available. Fruit shapes vary from small and round to ovoid, long, and skinny forms that can be a foot in length. Colors are equally variable: purple, green, red, white, striped, and even pink. Miniature varieties have been developed, which grow well in containers, even indoors. Once again, though, gardeners have come full circle—by far the most popular ornamental eggplant is the one whose small, pearly white fruits inspired the English name.

LOVE THOSE LOVE APPLES: THE TOMATO
(LYCOPERSICON ESCULENTUM MILL.)

You must have tomatoes if you have a summer garden here—fat, nearly obese, crimson things that have a wonderful weight in the hand. Dark, ripe tomatoes that, reeking with the sun, heat and land are the essence of summer and one of its chief joys. Of course, tomatoes!

Richard Goodman, *French Dirt: The Story of a Garden in the South of France*, 1991

Red, ripe, plump, delectable, and delightful, the tomato is the quintessential plant of the modern American vegetable garden. A vegetable garden, heaving with an overabundance of produce, can still be considered a failure if the tomatoes are scrawny or blighted. However, the tomato was very nearly a nonstarter in the race for most popular vegetable. As a matter of fact, the early history of the tomato in North America finds it planted firmly in the flowerbed, not in the vegetable garden.

The first Europeans to come into contact with tomatoes were the Spanish, who saw the plants, intermixed with maize and dahlias, growing in the floating gardens or *chinampas* of the Aztecs in Tenochtitlán (see Epilogue). The Spaniards noted that the Aztecs ate the *xitomatl* in a kind of salsa, a mixture of tomatoes, onions, and pulverized squash seeds.[20] When the explorers introduced the new plant to Europe, however, the public was not

WHAT'S IN A NAME

Tomato, *Lycopersicon*, "love apple," and "golden apple" are all names that have been applied at one time or another to that scraggly vined source of ketchup and spaghetti sauce. While an overabundance of *nom de plants* is nothing new in botany, the humble tomato has had more than its share.

Europeans inherited the tomato plant from the Aztecs and we derive the English term "tomato" from Náhuatl, the language of the Aztecs, who cultivated a plant they called *tomatl* or husk tomato (*Physalis ixocarpa* Hornem). When the wild South American ancestor of what we know today as the tomato (*Lycopersicon* sp.) arrived in Mexico, its fruits were probably only the size of the modern cherry tomato or even as small as grapes. However, during the domestication process, the fruit of *Lycopersicon* got larger than that of the original *tomatl*. Consequently, the Aztecs began to refer to *Lycopersicon* as *xitomatl* (big *tomatl*). Another common modern name of the *tomatl* is, ironically, *tomatillo* (little tomato).[1]

When the Spanish took the *xitomatl* to Europe, botanists were unsure what to call it. Pietro Matthiolo, a sixteenth-century Italian botanist and author of the earliest description of the tomato, coined the Italian name for the tomato—*pomi d'oro*, or "golden apple"—because the first specimen that he saw was yellow.[2] Since the red varieties followed hot on the heels of Matthiolo's golden apple, within a decade the name "love apple" (*poma amoris*) was being used in the rest of Europe, though the Italians continued to call tomatoes *pomi d'oro*. Matthiolo also accidentally gave the tomato its official genus name: *Lycopersicon*. The word is Latin for "wolf peach" and was the name given to a North African plant by the Roman herbalist and physician Galen (c. 130–201 C.E.). Matthiolo confused the New World tomato with the Old World *Lycopersicon*, and the connection stuck.

In America, "love apple" was the common name for *Lycopersicon* until people began to eat it. After that, "tomato" became the accepted and widely used name. So if you want to intrigue and infuriate your neighbors, talk loudly of the new, must-have ornamental you are growing in your garden—the winsome love apple. While your neighbors scour the nurseries for this enigmatic plant, you can eat the evidence.

1. J. A. Jenkins, "The Origin of the Cultivated Tomato," *Economic Botany* 2, no. 4 (1948): 389; David E. Williams, "A Review of Sources for the Study of Náhuatl Plant Classification," in *New Directions in the Study of Plants and People: Research Contributions from the Institute of Economic Botany*, vol. 8, ed. Ghillean T. Prance and Michael J. Balick (New York: New York Botanical Garden, 1990), 249–269.

2. Jenkins, "The Origins of the Cultivated Tomato," 380f.

convinced that the tomato was edible. Like the eggplant, the tomato or "love apple," as Europeans
called it, was a member of the deadly nightshade family and considered poisonous by most.

In 1728, Cambridge University botany professor
Richard Bradley wrote that the tomato "makes an
agreeable Plant to look at, but the Fruit . . . is dan-
gerous."[21] Olivier de Serres, agronomist to Henry IV
of France, noted that tomatoes were "marvelous
and golden" but "serve commonly to cover [our]
garden houses."[22] In his *Herbal*, John Gerard described
tomatoes as having a "ranke and stinking savour."[23]

The smell was noxious enough that many gardeners
recommended planting tomatoes far from the house.[24]

Eventually, some brave soul did eat one of the
love apple fruits. The Italians and Spanish were eating tomatoes by the early seventeenth century,
though another two centuries passed before they
were commonly eaten in England. In France, it would
take a revolution, literally, to make tomatoes a popular foodstuff. During the revolutionary period, a
French chef served "citizen tomatoes"—a patriotic
dish because of the tomatoes' bright red color and,
more important, because the aristocracy had never
been fond of them.[25]

In North America as well, the tomato had a
chilly reception. There is no evidence that the plant
was cultivated by the indigenous people of North
America; it probably immigrated with European
colonists. In French and Spanish settlements, tomatoes were readily accepted as a foodstuff from the
eighteenth century onward. Around the French settlement of New Orleans, tomato plants were described
as "bordering on the Mississippi swamp, spreading an
unusual length, forming a beautiful vine."[26]

English colonists were more hesitant in taking
to the tomato. Despite some early champions like
Thomas Jefferson, who was growing tomatoes at
Monticello by 1781, most Americans preferred
their tomatoes in their flowerbeds. Botanist James
Mapes said that the tomato was "long grown in our
gardens as an ornamental plant, under the name of
Love Apple, before being used at all as a culinary
vegetable. About 1827 or '28, we occasionally heard
of its being eaten in French or Spanish families, but

seldom if ever by others."[27] Outen Laws noted that "in 1803 only a few bushes of the tomato were grown in [the] flower garden, and their fruits were conspicuously arranged on the table, their 'bright hues attracting the admiration of the visitor.'"[28] It soon became widely known that the tomato was not poisonous, but even then, the taste still did not inspire much enthusiasm. As late as the mid-nineteenth century, tomatoes were described as "so fine with their sunny colors and so disappointing in taste."[29] From inauspicious beginnings, however, the tomato has flourished in both abundance and popularity.

These days most people grow tomatoes for their luscious fruit and not their appearance. Nevertheless, if you would like to enhance their beauty, here are a few ideas. Marigolds can add a touch of complementary color to your tomato patch. This artistic flair offers practical benefits as well: marigolds will entice bugs away from your precious plants. Or perhaps, follow the Aztec example and grow dahlias as a floral accompaniment to tomatoes. Many people are growing miniature varieties in containers or hanging baskets. To create a full, lush effect, select varieties that produce a lot of fruit. Finally, on a more whimsical note, consider using pink flamingos or other lawn ornaments as stakes for your tomato plants.

CHILI PEPPERS: THE BURNING BUSH
(CAPSICUM ANNUUM L.)

"Hot" really is the only adjective that one can use for chili peppers, the common name for the fruits of *Capsicum*. Hot colors, hot tastes, and a hot seller in the nursery, the chili pepper is the firecracker of the garden. The popularity of Mexican and South American cuisine has so ingrained this spice into the North American consciousness that salsa has surpassed ketchup as the preferred condiment. Chilies are now appreciated for subtle nuances of flavor, not just as a culinary powder keg. This chili revolution is not confined to the kitchen. Explosions of red, yellow, orange, green, and purple pointy fruits enliven garden borders and interior flowerpots. The ornamental pepper is even challenging the poinsettia for primacy as the *de rigueur* Christmas flower and decoration. The modern gardener is not the first to be lured by the chili's ornamental qualities. A seventeenth-century German bishop and innumerable Victorian gardeners grew this spicy bush as a beautiful curiosity long before they contemplated eating it.

The wild ancestor of the domesticated *Capsicum* had small, erect, bright red fruits that attracted birds, which dispersed its seed. The heat of chilies comes from the chemical capsaicin, which doesn't bother birds but does discourage most mammals from eating the fruits.[30] I don't know what the chili plant had against mammals, but capsaicin is a bit of evolutionary overkill. The chili, however, had not reckoned with the gutsy and foolhardy determination of

Piper Indicum medium longum erectum.

Piper Indicum maximum rotundum erectum.

how to play with fire.[31] Representations of chili pods decorate ancient pottery, textiles, and stele.[32] Chilies were and remain an integral part of the diet of the native peoples of Central and South America. Over thousands of years, each village developed its own preferred variety, which was slightly different and naturally superior in flavor to its neighbor's. From the five domesticated species of the *Capsicum* genus come thousands of pod shapes and sizes, a kaleidoscope of colors, and a heat index that ranges from the mundane bell pepper to the literally blistering habanero. *Capsicum annum* is the most common species and the source of nearly all the ornamental peppers. However, the other domesticated species also have their appeal.

Some varieties of the *rocoto* or *manzano* chili (*C. pubescens* Ruiz & Pav.) produce fruits that look exactly like miniature apples. Oh, the fun you could have with unsuspecting dinner guests! However, this species is difficult to cultivate in the United States, so it is not yet commonly available.[33] The *ají* chili (*C. baccatum* L.) is slightly better known and available commercially. 'Peri Peri' and 'Christmas Bell' are two cultivars with intriguing pod shapes that make interesting additions to any garden.[34] The tabasco pepper (*C. frutescens* L.) is the source of Louisiana's famous hot sauce, and marketers have made sure we see that little red pepper on everything from ballcaps to Christmas lights. The habanero or 'Scotch Bonnet' chilies belong to *Capsicum chinense* Jacq. Despite the botanical epithet, this species is native to the New World and, as

humans to add spice to their diet. Imagine the surprise of the first Native American to eat a wild chili—pretty, little berry . . . outrageous, burning pain! From that point, I'm sure the domestication of the chili was accomplished purely on a dare, as generation after generation sought to prove that they were undaunted by the eye-watering, tongue-scorching fruit.

Archaeologists continue to adjust the date of the earliest domestication of chilies. Certainly by 5000 B.C.E. humans had taken the first steps in learning one might guess, produces the hottest peppers.[35] Even the wild flea pepper or *chiltepín* (*C. annuum* var. *aviculare* [Dierb.] D'Arcy & Eshbaugh), long prized as a spice by the people of Sonora, has ornamental interest.[36] Of the domesticated species, *Capsicum annum* is the most variable, encompassing bell, banana, wax, paprika, pepperoncini, poblano, ancho, jalapeño, and hundreds of other pepper varieties. *C. annum* is also the most traveled, spreading from the New World to find a new home, first in Europe and then on every continent.[37]

Columbus returned to Europe with the chili in (presumably gloved) hand in the late fifteenth century. In 1613, apothecary Basilius Besler illustrated several chili plants growing in the garden of the Bishop of Eichstätt, intermixed with other exotic ornamentals.[38] Many Europeans considered the chili simply too hot to eat. "When we break but the skin, it sends out such a vapor into our lungs, as we fall all a coughing" is how Richard Lignon described the chili in his history of the island of Barbados published in 1657.[39] Many early references to chili focus on its medicinal, not culinary, properties. Chili added a kick to many patent medicines.[40] In the eighteenth century, cayenne, as the dried powdered chili came to be known, became more accepted as a spice. The Hungarians are probably the most famous converts, with paprika peppers becoming part of their national identity as a crucial ingredient in their national dish, goulash. The chili also became popular in the cuisines of India, Thailand, Africa, and Asia, spreading around the world by 1600.[41] Despite their culinary acceptance, bushes of chilies remained a popular ornamental in England and America throughout the nineteenth century.[42] A particularly popular ornamental cultivar, 'Child's Celestial,' is mentioned by several authors as producing a beautiful, abundant mix of bright red and deep golden pods on a small, compact bush.[43]

While the ornamental 'Child's Celestial' pepper was still being sold in the first decade of the twentieth century, as the century progressed the aesthetic qualities of chilies changed. For example, I found no mention of decorating with chilies in either the war or victory garden literature. Perhaps the new culinary varieties were less appealing because the fruits usually hung down and were more likely to be hidden by the foliage. It was not until the early 1990s that chilies made a real ornamental comeback. Once again, bright yellow and red fruits provided fireworks in the garden. Ornamental peppers also worked well as container plants, ripening and holding their colors indoors throughout the fall. The red and green combination made them a natural choice for a decorative Christmas plant and as December wedding flowers. Over the last few years, a full spectrum of colors, from bright yellow to black-purple, and pods in every size and shape ensure many new combinations for the garden. In the new millennium, a completely "hotless" ornamental pepper has been bred, apparently in response to children making the same discovery that Native Americans made about seven thousand years ago—pretty, red fruit . . . HOT! Enough said.[44]

A turnip might have been going too far, but he'd never have known a cabbage from a carnation.
Independent on Sunday, November 24, 1996

A FLOWERING CABBAGE THAT DOESN'T FLOWER AND ISN'T A CABBAGE

If one wishes to be pedantic, ornamental cabbage isn't cabbage; it's kale. Technically, cabbages are the members of *Brassica oleracea* that form a series of tightly pressed overlapping leaves around a terminal bud or, in other words, form a head. In fact the English name "cabbage" is from the Old French *caboche*, which means "head." Kale, on the other hand, doesn't form a head and has a tendency to be a taller plant. So the rosette of ornamental cabbage is simply a squashed kale plant, though naturally it doesn't look like kale.

While it might have been simpler and more artistic to adopt the Japanese name *habotan*, the powers that be decided to call the plant ornamental cabbage or flowering cabbage. The only difficulty with the latter name is that the flowering cabbage doesn't flower—at least not in the first year—because it is a biennial. Moreover, technically the name "flowering cabbage" was already in use. The "cauli" in cauliflower is a medieval corruption of the Roman word for cabbage. On the other hand, ornamental kales, like 'Redbor,' are truly kales and, thankfully, actually look like kales.

It hardly seems a wise marketing move to name these frilly, decorative plants "cabbage," but I can only suppose that the alternatives were worse. By the late twentieth century, many people had forgotten about kale as a vegetable, which would have left collards as the most appropriate common name. While I am a huge fan of those Southern greens, trying to convince the general American public that collards are fanciful and colorful might have daunted even the most skilled advertising agent. Nineteenth-century seedsmen had similar difficulty trying to sell their kale seeds, a vegetable known for more than two thousand years by that time and not likely to inspire much enthusiasm. To attract buyers, they took to describing their kale as the latest variety from some exotic locale. In doing so, they incurred the scorn of a botanist who, noting that the old Jerusalem kale was now being called Siberian, stated:

It has also been called Prussian, Russian, Hungarian, and Manchester. If someone had called it a collard or colewort, there would have been no buyers, but a foreign kale was a dead cert. Yet if it was sold under the name Hiersolymatanian Kale and a tale invented that it was found in the Pacha's garden in Lebanon, . . . or it was called Ptolemaic Kale and said to have been found in the folds of a mummy, so that its pedigree might be traced up to the pottage of the Pharoahs [demand would have been enormous].[1]

Perhaps, in preference to Hiersolymatanian Kale, ornamental cabbage isn't that bad a name after all.

1. Dr. Lindley, *Gardener's Chronicle*, 20 June 1846; reprinted in William W. Valk, "Siberian Kale," *The Horticulturist* 3, no. 3 (8 August 1848): 148–149.

CARNATION? CABBAGE?
NOPE, COLLARDS:
ORNAMENTAL CABBAGE AND KALE
(BRASSICA OLERACEA L. [ACEPHALA GROUP])

Of all the modern ornamental vegetables, no transformation has been as dramatic as the humble kale into the magnificent flowering cabbage. And I don't just mean appearance, though that certainly has been spectacular. Modern ornamental eggplant and chilies are simply a rediscovery of a past tradition. Sweetpotato vine probably has a long history of being used as an ornamental trailer. The new cultivars are simply a logical extension of that process. However, for people in America and Europe to seek out an ornamental for their flowerbeds with cabbage in its name (see "A Flowering Cabbage That Doesn't Flower and Isn't a Cabbage") is truly astounding, because few plants have a more mundane reputation than the cabbage.

The species *Brassica oleracea* is a bit of a botanical overachiever. Cabbage, kale, broccoli, cauliflower, kohlrabi, collards, and all their varieties are various forms of that singular species. The wild ancestor, which looks more like kale than cabbage, is found along the Atlantic coast of Europe and was probably domesticated by the late Bronze Age.[45] Greek and Roman writers were familiar with several different varieties, including possibly an early kohlrabi and broccoli.[46] According to classical mythology, the cabbage arose from the tears of King Lycurgus, who had murdered his son after being driven mad by Dionysus. Hence, cabbages were used as a remedy for drunkenness, and the cabbage and grape were never to be grown near each other.[47] On a happier note, Emperor Diocletian abandoned the tribulations of Roman politics in 305 C.E. and returned to his native Croatia, content to grow cabbages in his retirement.[48]

From the collapse of the Roman Empire through the Dark Ages and the Renaissance to the modern day, cabbage and kale have been mainstays of the European vegetable garden. However, cabbage was never a very glamorous inhabitant. European writers often noted the malodorous emanations from the plant and its rather frumpy appearance.[49] The comments of John Parkinson are typical: "The many different scents that arise from the herbes, as Cabbages, Onions &c, are scarce well pleasing to perfume the lodgings of any house; and the many overtures and breaches as it were of many of the beds thereof, which must necessarily bee, are as little pleasing to the sight."[50] To see cabbage as an ornamental was simply beyond the imaginative powers of most English and American gardeners. Most would have sympathized with the surprise of Edwin, Lord Weeks, who in 1894 visited a formal garden in the town of Shiraz in what became Iran. There he noted "the gardener, probably for his own domestic needs, had ornamented one of these walks by a border of cabbages, with highly decorative effect."[51] Needless to say, Lord Weeks's discovery never caught on.

Kale, on the other hand, seems to have struck a more pleasing note with the European gardening aesthetic. The crinkled foliage of its arched, drooping

FIG. 8-5
A Chinese poem about cabbage inspired Gion Nankai (1677–1751) to create this calligraphy scroll. The poem can be roughly translated: "Cramped yet without hindrance in my thatched hut. Content in poverty, I enjoy the scent of cabbage."
Japanese, Edo period, 18th century
Hanging scroll, ink on paper, 110.1 x 25.5 cm
Freer Gallery of Art, Smithsonian Institution, Washington, D.C., Gift of Kurt A. Gitter in memory of Harold P. Stern

FIG. 8-6
Enid A. Haupt Garden, Smithsonian
Institution, Washington, D.C., 1989
Smithsonian Institution, Horticulture
Services Division, photo: Weinstein

leaves received approving comments. Because it is taller than the squat cabbage, it could be used as a sedate background to more colorful flowers. What is unclear is when exactly this idea of kale as an ornamental originated. I can trace it back to no earlier than the late nineteenth century, but the possibility certainly exists that it is much older.[52] Yet, for two millennia the Europeans overlooked a unique ornamental potential of kale that was discovered by the Japanese.

In the 1700s, kale was introduced into Japan, but the Japanese were not overly fond of its flavor. Over the next one hundred years or so, Japanese gardeners transformed the humble kale into the extravagant ornamental cabbage by selecting out the occasional colorful mutation in its leaves. The

Japanese called their creation *habotan*, which translates as "leaf peony." The tight rosette of white, purple, or pink frilled leaves surrounded by dark green does bear a certain resemblance to that showy flower. *Habotan* became a requisite autumnal planting in many parts of Japan, providing little splashes of color in gardens and yards during the shortening days of the year. The Japanese also used *habotan* indoors, arranging them in containers like flowers.[53]

Sometime in the early twentieth century, *habotan* was reintroduced into Europe and America, apparently under the name "drumhead kale."[54] However, it didn't really catch on as an ornamental until the 1990s.[55] Professional horticulturists and amateur gardeners discovered that ornamental cabbage, as it was now being called, was an ideal plant to provide color in the fall—and colors there are in abundance! The Japanese have also continued to develop new varieties. At one end of the spectrum are the green-and-white 'Kamone,' which are so tightly ruffled as to look like cauliflower or broccoli from a distance. Less crinkled are the 'Osaka' and 'Tokyo' varieties, but what they lack in wrinkles, they make up for in color. Bright pink centers, surrounded by purplish-gray or green foliage, definitely can enhance a winter landscape. Now, of course, it is difficult to pass any professionally maintained landscape without spotting at least the occasional ornamental cabbage, though more often than not, if you see one, you will in fact see masses of them. They have even filled the Victorian parterre at the Smithsonian Castle in Washington, D.C., though at least one Victorian was explicitly opposed to the

SWEETPOTATO OR YAM?

If you grew up in the South, as I did, you are probably familiar with the many incarnations of sweetpotato in soufflés, pies, and biscuits. Many Americans are unaware that the candied yams of their Thanksgiving dinners are in fact sweetpotatoes. If you are in doubt, check the label of the candied yams that you buy in the supermarket. You will discover that the United States Department of Agriculture (USDA) has required the inclusion of "sweetpotatoes" somewhere on the label. By the way, it is also the USDA that proclaimed the correct spelling of sweetpotato as one word, not two.

Sweetpotatoes and yams are two different species and not even very closely related to each other or to the humble spud. Yams belong to the genus *Dioscorea*, found around the world but primarily in West Africa. In fact, Nigeria produces more yams than any other nation. The native peoples of West Africa domesticated the yam five thousand years ago. By the time the Portuguese made contact with that area in the fifteenth century, yams were already an important staple. The local name for the plant was *niam*, which became *ynhame* in Portuguese, and eventually "yam" in English.[1]

True yams were never very popular in the United States though they were and are grown in the Caribbean. The confusion with the sweetpotato dates to the 1930s, when farmers in the South developed a darker, sweeter sweetpotato that they called yams.

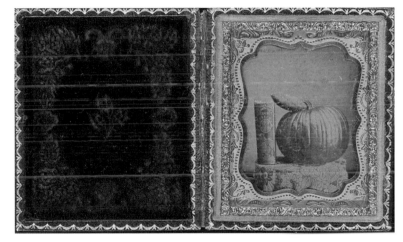

Pumpkin, Sweet Potato and Book, artist unidentified, c. 1855 Smithsonian American Art Museum, Museum purchase from the Charles Isaacs Colletion made possible in part by the Luisita L. and Franz H. Denghausen Endowment

1. Edward S. Ayenus and D. G. Coursey, "The Botany, Ethnobotany, Use and Possible Future of Yams in West Africa," *Economic Botany* 26, no. 4 (1972): 301.

idea. George W. Johnston in his *History of English Gardening* thought that the kitchen garden should be "kept in the appropriate beauty of order and neatness; without any extravagant attempt at ornament by the mingling of useless trees, or planting its Cabbages, &c. in waving lines."[56]

A bit of Victorian prudishness toward cabbages is creeping back into the modern garden literature. At least twice, the *Washington Post* garden writers have tried to banish ornamental cabbage from the "must have" shopping list, while another writer described them as "pimples" on the landscape.[57] Like all hot trends, a backlash is only to be expected. Still, it appears that ornamental cabbage is here to stay and is slowly being transformed into a flower in its own right. It is even making its way into the florists' shops and the occasional bridal bouquet.

SWEETPOTATO: THE ORIGINAL POTATO
(*IPOMOEA BATATAS* [L.] LAM.)

Sweetpotato vine is a recent addition to the horticultural palette of ornamental vegetables, but the plant itself has had a long and illustrious history. Sweetpotato tubers decorated Peruvian pottery, rescued the Chinese from famine, commanded a high price as an aphrodisiac in Shakespeare's England, and were prized by Napoleon's Josephine. The most important food crop of the morning glory family, over seventeen thousand varieties of sweetpotatoes are grown around the world. And yet many Americans know it only as a misnamed side dish at their Thanksgiving dinner (see "Sweetpotato or Yam?").

The sweetpotato was first domesticated in South America, probably somewhere along the coast of Peru, as early as ten thousand years ago. Sweetpotato was part of a constellation of crops, including potatoes, beans, avocados, *achira* or edible canna (see "Achira"), manioc, peanuts, peppers, and squash. It was important enough, though, to be included in burial offerings as well as being portrayed on pottery and textiles.[58]

From South America, the sweetpotato spread throughout the world. It initially spread to Central America, southern North America, and into the Caribbean basin. While it did not become an important staple in these areas, the Maya of the Yucatán Peninsula included sweetpotato in a group of plants described as "essential, some holy and all very old."[59] More surprising, the sweetpotato hopped the Pacific.

Based on similarities in the indigenous names for sweetpotato in South America and some Pacific islands, scientists have hypothesized a prehistoric journey for the sweetpotato from South America to the Marquesas, Society, and Cook Islands of the Pacific. Exactly when and how that transfer took place is not known. The Maori of New Zealand were probably cultivating sweetpotatoes as early as the fourteenth century. The Maori name for sweetpotato is *kumara*, which is very similar to a common South American name. Based on Maori lore, if the sweetpotatoes were growing poorly, farmers would place wooden *kumara* gods and dried human heads in their fields to improve the yield.[60]

Europeans were responsible for the sweetpotato's other journeys. In 1492, Columbus saw the plant in cultivation in Haiti and returned to Spain with it the next year. It was planted in the royal gardens and given the name *batata*. "Batata" is obviously the precursor to the English word potato. In fact, sweetpotato was the original potato of England, having beaten the humble spud to Europe by fifty years.[61] From Europe, the Portuguese introduced the *batata* to Africa, India, and the East Indics. In the sixteenth and seventeenth centuries, the Spanish also transported the sweetpotato from Mexico west to the Philippines.

The sweetpotato reached China from the Philippines in a rather unusual way. In 1593, the Chinese province of Fujian was devastated by a famine. Kin Hozeng, Governor of Fujian, sent a mission to the Philippines for food plants to help feed the populace. His ambassadors returned the following year with sweetpotatoes. The Chinese still cultivate them under the name *faan shue* or "foreign tuber."[62] The Japanese imported the sweetpotato from China. It became such an important crop to the inhabitants of the Ryukyu Islands that they issued a stamp in 1955 to commemorate the 350th anniversary of the sweetpotato's introduction.[63]

While the rest of the world considered sweetpotatoes a prolific source of food, the English were interested in the vegetable for another reason. Influenced by the shape of the tuber, the English believed the sweetpotato was a powerful aphrodisiac. They consumed it both as a vegetable and as a candied sweet known as "sucket." Shakespeare even took note of the vegetable's wanton reputa-

tion. In *The Merry Wives of Windsor*, the jovial Falstaff states, "Let the sky rain potatoes; let it thunder to the tune of Green sleeves, hail kissing-comfits, and snow eryngoes; let there come a tempest of provocation, I will shelter me here." Eryngoes, the candied roots of sea holly, comfits, and sweetpotatoes were all popular aphrodisiacs of the period.[64]

Sweetpotato, however, was a luxury available only to the wealthy of Stuart England because the English were never very successful in cultivating sweetpotato. The common vegetables of that time, such as carrots, cabbage, and leeks, were annuals grown from seed.[65] The sweetpotato does not produce flowers or seeds when grown north of about 25 degrees latitude and has to be propagated from slips, small pieces of vine, or by using the roots.[66] Herbalist John Gerard did grow it in his garden in the late sixteenth century, though he was puzzled by the lack of flowers and could only watch as the plants and roots rotted when the weather turned cold.[67] Therefore the tubers had to be imported from Spain, which led to elaborate precautions being taken to protect the valuable aphrodisiacs. For example, when Lord Spencer hosted a banquet for King Charles I, he hired a special porter to guard a box of sweetpotatoes being transported from London to his country estate.[68]

It is not surprising then that the more amenable Peruvian potato enjoyed even greater popularity in Europe and eventually took over the common name of potato. The adjective "sweet" was added to the older, original potato to differentiate it. The sweetpotato had only one brief resurgence in popularity

FIG. 8-7
Marion Feasting the British Officer on Sweet Potatoes, George Washington Mark, 1848
National Gallery of Art, Washington, D.C.
Gift of Edgar William and Bernice Chrysler Garbisch

their guerrilla campaign against the British.

According to a popular legend, after General Marion met with a British officer to discuss a prisoner exchange, he invited the officer to share his dinner of roasted sweetpotatoes. When the British leader saw his dinner, he declared that if the Americans were willing to subsist on nothing but roots, he did not see how they could be defeated. The officer's comments are rather ironic. A few hundred years earlier, his ancestors would have considered sweetpotatoes a luxurious delicacy. They would have thought Marion was feeding his troops on caviar as opposed to humble roots.

Ornamental Sweetpotato Vine

In the northern latitudes, sweetpotato will not set flowers. Its ornamental appeal is in its foliage. People have long been aware that if you put a small chunk of sweetpotato in a glass of water, it will produce a long vine with bright, heart-shaped leaves. (This won't work if the sweetpotato is already candied!) The vines can be trained around windows, and I remember them being a common sight in our kitchen when I was a child.

Around 1995, two spectacular new varieties of sweetpotato vine appeared. They were both originally being grown for the tuber. However, while they may not have tasted great, they were beautiful to look at. The first to appear was 'Blackie' with its dark purple, almost black foliage. Shortly thereafter 'Margarita' was discovered growing in a garden in Raleigh, North Carolina, and subsequently developed by horticulturists at the University of Georgia.

in Europe under the patronage of Empress Josephine, the first wife of Napoleon. Josephine was a Creole and very fond of sweetpotatoes. She served them regularly at imperial festivities and, for a short time, sweetpotatoes were all the rage. However, their popularity did not survive even to the end of her short reign.[69]

In the United States, sweetpotatoes are associated primarily with the culture and cuisine of the South. Early English colonists grew it in the Southern colonies. Thomas Jefferson was well familiar with it at his farm at Monticello. However, it is another Revolutionary War figure with whom sweetpotatoes are more usually associated. General Francis Marion, the "Swamp Fox" of South Carolina, and his troops were said to have survived on sweetpotatoes during

'Margarita' has bright, almost Day-Glo, chartreuse foliage. Both cultivars have become extremely popular in the world of ornamental gardening.[70] They are fast growing and can provide quick ground cover, or if used in a more restrained manner, can provide effective accents. They can even brighten up container plantings. With seventeen thousand varieties of sweetpotato in cultivation around the planet, it probably won't be long until new varieties of ornamental sweetpotato vine make their appearance.

LESS WELL-KNOWN ORNAMENTAL VEGETABLES

Looking around your flower garden, you might be surprised by how many of your ornamental plants or their near relatives are considered edible in different cultures. Or maybe the recent success of ornamental sweetpotato vine, peppers, and eggplant might encourage you to venture a little wider for the new and unusual in your garden.

Achira (*Canna edulis* Ker Gawl.)

In the Apurimac valley of the Andes, Peruvian villagers cultivate a plant for use in a local Christian celebration, the Corpus Christi Festival. They call the plant *achira* and *p'asna jikichi*, which means the "fruit that makes girls hiccup." They collect its fleshy rhizomes and bake them in large pits dug into the ground. When the roots are cooked, they collect them and sell them to other villages as part of the festival. The plant is *Canna edulis* and is

Canna Indica lutea rubris maculis punctata.

FIG. 8-8
Another American exotic grown as an ornamental in the Bishop of Eichstätt's garden was the canna. This is probably *Canna indica*, not the edible species, *C. edulis*.
Reprinted with permission from *The Garden at Eichstätt*, Benedikt Taschen Verlag

closely related to the popular ornamental canna (*Canna indica* L.), which is cultivated today for its striking flowers. *Achira*, though, has an ancient history. Based on archaeological finds and its representation on pottery, we can trace *achira* to approximately 4,500 years ago. Moreover, it is possible that the modern Corpus Christi Festival is a transformation of a much older Incan festival called *Inti Raymi*.[71] In Europe, the canna was admired for its flowers, and it graced the gardens at Louis XIV's palace at Versailles.

Lablab bean (*Lablab purpureus* (L.) Sweet)
The beautiful purple pods of the hyacinth bean (also
called bonavist and field wal) make a natural choice
for an attractive ornamental vine. The native peoples
of Angola eat a variety with very tender pods that
they call *macululu*. In Egypt, hyacinth bean or
lablab has been used to make cakes called *taamiah*
when broad beans are in scarce supply. Hyacinth
bean is also eaten in India, where it is recorded in
ancient descriptions of royal feasts.[72] Peoples of the
Caribbean eat it much like pigeon peas. When the
hyacinth bean was introduced into Brazil in the
1960s, it took a concerted campaign by one man,
Reimar von Schaafhausen, to convince local farmers
to grow it. While it never really caught on as a food,

it did become a popular forage crop for cattle. More
interestingly, von Schaafhausen exchanged seeds of
another ornamental food plant, Job's Tears, for his
first specimens of *lablab* from Angola.[73]

Job's Tears or Adlay (*Coix lacryma-jobi* L.)
Job's Tears cannot really be considered a common
ornamental grass in the United States, though it is
grown at the gardens of the Smithsonian Institution.
The most striking feature of Job's Tears is its stone-
like fruits, which, when ripe, have a polished
appearance. They are commonly worn as beads on
necklaces and other jewelry and they have even
been used to make rosaries. The people of northeastern India cultivate a soft kernel variety that
they shell and eat like peanuts. This variety is a key
ingredient in an alcoholic beverage called *magharu*.
Job's Tears was cultivated extensively by the native
peoples of Mongolia and ancient China.[74]

Ceylon spinach or Vine spinach (*Basella alba* L.)
Ceylon spinach originated somewhere in southern
Asia. Its leaves are eaten throughout the tropics but
are especially popular in India and the Philippines.
While Ceylon spinach can be grown in temperate
regions, it has not become popular as a food.
Instead, people preferred to grow it as an attractive
ornamental vine under the name basella or malabar
nightshade. Europeans had known of the plant since
the seventeenth century and, as trade routes expanded,
they introduced it to the South Sea Islands. There, a
white ornamental variety was developed. Basella
did not make an appearance in the United States

until 1899, when nurserymen tried to sell it as a summer vegetable and ornamental arbor vine.[75]

Okra (*Abelmoschus esculentus* (L.) Moench)
Okra, gumbo, or lady fingers was probably domesticated in India, though the recent discovery of a second edible variety in West Africa has reopened the debate that it originated in tropical Africa.[76] Over the last thousand years, okra has spread throughout the world, first by the expanding Muslim empire and then by the growth of European colonial empires. People have toyed with the idea of okra as an ornamental vegetable for the last fifty years or so. When Americans were contemplating ways to make their victory gardens more attractive, okra was a vegetable that many authors noted as having ornamental possibilities. Because okra is in the hibiscus family, naturally gardeners first appreciated the showy cream-colored flowers with dark accents. Dried okra pods were also considered ideal for avant-garde flower arrangements. Many authors noted the particular beauty of the 'White Velvet' cultivar, whose long white pods were very striking. 'White Velvet' okra can still be found, but it is the red-podded varieties that seem to have captured the most ornamental interest recently.

Jícama or yam bean (*Pachyrhizus* sp.)
Jícama is considered neither a common vegetable nor ornamental in the United States. However, if you are looking for something unusual it might be worth a try. Jícama is a venerable vegetable with a long history in Mesoamerica. It is one of the Aztec

crops grown in the *chinampas*. A member of the bean family, its pods and leaves are poisonous. It is the large root that is eaten; hence its other name: Mexican turnip. It grows as a creeping vine, which produces many bunches of blue and white flowers.

Balsam apple (*Momordica balsamina* L.)
Exotic, unusual Christmas ornaments, that's what I thought when I first glimpsed the pale-lime, warty, pointed balsam apple fruits hanging on a wire fence. But Hallmark has never created a Christmas ornament that explodes to reveal slimy, blood-red seeds. Throughout Asia, the immature fruits of the balsam apple are a pickled delicacy. Americans, for the most part, have simply been confused by it. Thomas Jefferson planted it in his flower garden. Raphaelle Peale included it in a painting of fruits, while his uncle James Peale included it in a vegetable composition.

Beefsteak mint or Perilla
(*Perilla frutescens* (L.) Britton)

Perilla is a member of the mint family that is native to Asia and was once a commonly grown vegetable in ancient China. It is mentioned in agricultural treatises dating to the Han dynasty (206 B.C.E.–219 C.E.), and in the fifth-century *Qiminyaoshu* it is listed as a common vegetable. However, in modern China it is grown only occasionally as a medicinal plant.[77] In America it has found a home as an ornamental. Its flowers are inconspicuous, but it produces striking purple or green fuzzy leaves that are wavy and deeply incised. These leaves make perilla an attractive and colorful accent plant.

Curled mallow (*Malva verticillata* L.)

Another old Chinese vegetable is curled mallow or *kuei* as it is known in the ancient texts. Unlike perilla, it is often classified as an invasive weed in the United States, though it occasionally appears in gardens. Curled mallow was the most important leafy green vegetable to the ancient Chinese, predating the rise of Chinese cabbage by several centuries. During the Han dynasty, it usually rated its own chapter in agricultural treatises. At the time of *Qiminyaoshu*, several varieties were cultivated, including purple- and white-stemmed ones. In Ming dynasty China, cultivation of curled mallow had been all but forgotten, replaced by Chinese cabbage.[78] Sometimes reaching five feet with small flowers, the plant is a tall, scraggly affair, but is such an august vegetable that it might be worth growing in your garden just for the historical interest.

Water hawthorn or Waterbloometjie
(*Aponogeton distachyos* L.)

Vegetables are not only grown on dry land. In South Africa, the San bushman collect the flowers and stems of the water hawthorn and eat them like asparagus or string beans. This fragrant aquatic has become very popular among modern Afrikaners as an ingredient in stews, and has even inspired folk songs. Overharvesting depleted the wild populations, but it is now grown commercially and can be bought frozen or canned. *Waterbloometjie* is a beautiful plant. Lance-shaped leaves float on the water, smelling of hawthorn. Thin shoots arise from the leaves and produce a bundle of small flowers enclosed in snowy white bracts. This adaptable plant has been naturalized in at least one river in southern France for the last one hundred and fifty years.[79] There are many other aquatic vegetables, such as water spinach (*Ipomoea aquatica* Forsskal) and purple loosestrife (*Lythrum salicaria* L.). Unfortunately, they are classed as noxious weeds and their importation and cultivation are forbidden in the United States.

Ornamental onions (*Allium* sp.)

The *Allium* genus is widespread across temperate Eurasia, Africa, and North America. Of the six hundred or so species, nearly all are edible and many have been long domesticated. Bulb onions, shallots, garlic, chives, and leeks are just a few of the culinary species. Many species of *Allium* have been grown as ornamentals since the Renaissance. Popular modern ornamental species are *A. roseum* L. (rose flowered garlic) and *A. moly* L. (golden garlic). Many

Marrubium Creticum angustifolium. Malua crispa. Pseudsdictamus floribus verticillatis.

Balsamina foemina.

Momordica fructu luteo rubescente. Balsamina Mas fructu punicea.

gardeners combine beauty with utility, admiring the flowers of their chives or the blue-green foliage of leeks, before harvesting for the table.[80]

Swiss chard (*Beta vulgaris* L.)

Swiss chard is the same species as the more commonly known garden beet; however, these plants have been bred for edible leaves, not for a large root. Many people are now familiar with the modern ornamental forms of 'Rhubarb Chard' (with bright red stems and leaf veins), 'Bright Lights' (with yellow stems), and 'Rainbow Chard,' a mixture of red, green, and yellow stems. These are not the products of white-coated scientists in laboratories, modifying the humble beet's genetic code to create Frankenstein plants.

Nope, it just seems to be something the beet likes to do. Aristotle knew about the red variety in 350 B.C.E. In the nineteenth century, Swiss chard was much admired for its colored stems and wavy leaves and marketed as an ornamental under the name 'Chilean beet.' Red, yellow, white, silver, and green stems were all there and prized as novelties in the flower garden.[81]

Carrot (*Daucus carota* L.)

The carrot is an Old World vegetable that probably originated in Afghanistan. It was introduced into northern Europe via Turkey in the thirteenth or fourteenth century. The wild form has a small purplish or yellowish root that was not transformed into the more familiar long orange form until the seventeenth century, when the Dutch created the Horn varieties.[82] English colonists brought it to North America, where the carrot escaped the garden and began to grow wild along the roadsides. There it is known as Queen Anne's Lace, whose delicate clusters of white flowers are a perfectly acceptable addition to any wildflower garden. In addition to the flowers, the feathery foliage of Queen Anne's Carrot (as I think we should call it) is becoming more popular as a background planting. In 1629, John Parkinson remarked on the parallel with feathers in describing an unusual fashion trend of his time: "The carot hath many winged leaves . . . of a deep green colour, some whereof in autumn will turn to be of a fine red or purple (the beauty whereof allureth many Gentlewomen often times to gather the leaves, and stick them in their hats or heads, or pin them on their arm instead of feathers)."[83]

Asparagus (*Asparagus officinalis* L.)

Known in its cultivated form since the early days of the Roman Empire, asparagus has graced the mosaics of Pompeii and inspired Monet. It is one of the few vegetable perennials. The edible portions are immature stems that must be harvested by hand. If the stems are not harvested, the asparagus produces very tall feathery foliage, which is quite beautiful. A closely related species from South Africa, *A. densiflorus* (Kunth) Jessop, is also grown as an ornamental under the name asparagus fern. Culinary asparagus is becoming an ornamental vegetable in its own right with the development of a new purple variety. In the 1980s, researchers in California used a strain of asparagus from Italy to breed disease resistance into their varieties. While that was not successful, they did generate deep burgundy spears of asparagus. Making lemonade from lemons, they developed their new strain (which also happened to be very tasty), named it 'Purple Passion,' and released it on the open market.[84]

The showy leaves of Rhubarb Chard can be used effectively in flower arrangements. Both surfaces are attractively crumpled and the brilliant leaf stalks add a striking note of color.

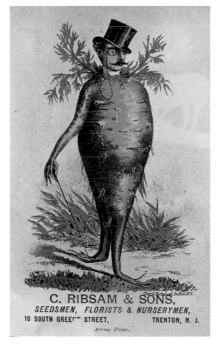

C. RIBSAM & SONS,
SEEDSMEN, FLORISTS & NURSERYMEN,
10 SOUTH GREEN STREET,   TRENTON, N. J.

FIG. 8-14
'Rhubarb Chard'
Reprinted from *Vegetable Gardening in Color*, Daniel J. Foley

FIG. 8-15
Advertising card from C. Ribsam & Sons, Trenton, New Jersey
Smithsonian Institution, Horticulture Services Division

EPILOGUE
An Aztec Garden of Ornamental Vegetables

Based purely on the number of ornamental vegetables grown, surely the prize for the most beautiful vegetable garden must go to the Aztecs. Tomatoes, sweetpotatoes, and peppers were all grown in their gardens that seemed to float upon a lake. Over one hundred years before Fouquet held his ill-fated fête at Vaux-le-Vicomte, Europeans saw for the first time how beautiful a vegetable garden could be.

When Spanish explorer Hernán Cortés (1485–1547) arrived on the Yucatán coast in 1519, he was told tales of a great city beyond the western mountains. The city was Tenochtitlán, the capital of the mighty Aztec empire, ruled by Motecuhzoma II (Montezuma). He dispatched emissaries with gifts of gold, feathered headdresses, and food to greet the strangers. The Spanish declined the tortillas, avocados, guavas, turkey eggs, and *zapotas* fruits, because they had been blessed with the splattered blood of a human sacrifice. The gold, however, was much appreciated, and it confirmed what the Spanish had known for the last twenty years—that abundant riches lay to the west.[1]

Cortés marched his army inland from the coast, scaled the mountains, and looked down into the Valley of Mexico. There they saw a long shallow lake spread throughout the basin, rimmed by volcanoes. On an island in that turquoise lake was the magnificent city of Tenochtitlán. Tall stone pyramids rose from its center and broad bridges and causeways linked it to the shore. Surrounding the city and along the edges of the lake were gardens, transected by canals, busy with canoes and people. Upon seeing them for the first time, the Spaniards thought the gardens floated—verdant flotsam on a crystal lake, glittering in the sun. They had never seen anything quite like it, but the sight only made them more eager to seek the city's riches. They marched down the mountains into the valley, across the bridges, and into the capital. Within a few years of Cortés's arrival, Motecuhzoma II was dead, his people were conquered, and his empire was no more.

The beautiful lake gardens of the Aztecs survived, however. The gardens can still be seen in a few locations, most notably at Xochimilco on the outskirts of modern Mexico City. The plants, including vegetables, that the Aztecs grew many centuries ago have found homes in gardens all over the world, but the gardens of the lake surely must have been some of the most beautiful homes that vegetables have ever had.

FIG. 9-1
Floating Gardens at Xochimilco, Mexico City, Mexico, 1920s–1930s
Smithsonian Institution, Archives of American Gardens, Garden Club of America Collection, photo: Edward Van Altena

FIG. 9-2

"Mexicani, Quomodo a suo Deunculo sev idolo primumducti fuerint," Theodor de Bry (1528–1598), *Historia Americae sive Novi Orbis, Part Nine*, 1602
Engravings such as this one from the first decade of the seventeenth century supported the European misconception that the *chinampas* were free-floating gardens. In fact, this image tells a story from Aztec mythology. When the Aztecs arrived in the Valley of Mexico, they paid tribute to the ruling king, who demanded that maize and vegetables be grown on a floating platform and delivered to his palace.
The Library of Congress

Archaeologists are not sure when the gardens were first planted in the basin lakes of the Valley of Mexico. It may have been as early as two thousand years ago. They were certainly a well-established horticultural tradition when the ancestors of the Aztecs migrated into the valley in the thirteenth century.[2] Nevertheless, it is from the Aztec language Náhuatl that we derive the modern name *chinampas*, which translates simply as "raised beds surrounded by fences."

Chinampas were not vegetable gardens per se; nor did they float. They were an intensive, highly productive, agricultural system of plant beds in shallow lake water, "swamps gardens," as one author rather unpoetically termed them.[3] In rectangular plots of approximately 30 meters long by 2.5 meters wide, the Aztecs cultivated maize, vegetables, fruits, flowers, and medicinal plants all together. Woven wattle fences marked the boundaries and supported the sides of the beds. Mud scooped out from the edges and piled in the middle created ditches along the sides that eventually flowed into larger canals. Over time, *chinampas* were raised higher and higher above the surrounding waterways. Willow trees were planted along the edges. Their roots grew together and further stabilized the beds, while the tops were pruned into narrow, delicate forms, resembling Lombardy poplars.[4] The rich mud and compost allowed farmers to produce crop after crop throughout the year, providing food and flowers to the growing population of ancient Tenochtitlán.[5]

Most of the foodstuffs grown on *chinampas* are familiar: maize, beans, squash, chilies, onions, tomatoes, sweetpotatoes, and peanuts. Other vegetables, perhaps less well known, included amaranth, jícama, *tomatillos*, and cacti, the pads of which were a popular food. Interspersed among all these vegetables were bright flowers. Dahlias, poinsettias, salvias, lupines, marigolds, zinnias, cosmos, tiger lilies, and many other popular modern ornamentals are all native to Mexico.[6] Another name for garden was simply *xochitla* or "flower place."[7] Flowers were offered at the yearly ritual blessing of the *chinampas* in a ceremony known as *xochimanaloya*.[8] Besides fertility, flowers were closely associated with the Aztec idea of beauty. *Xochipilli*, Young Lord of Flowers, was also the patron of poetry and song. In Náhuatl the word for poetry was "flower speech."[9] Cecile Hulse Matschat described the bright beauty of the *chinampas* of Xochimilco in the early twentieth century:

It seems as though all the flowers in the world must grow at Xochimilco. Lavender, purple, and white stocks cover whole islands. There are fields of scarlet poppies, sweet peas, and marguerites; acres of orange marigolds, thousands of lilies, and pink ivy-geraniums that clamber and climb. Large single violets, odorous and long-stemmed. . . . Chrysanthemums edge the garden plots; roses make dense jungles among the sugar cane; and shy little pansies, cream, yellow, and black, turn their faces skyward. Here at the water's edge are hundreds of callas, each one seemingly afloat upon the black water, and in the background a palm-thatched hut smothered in nasturtiums, orange and yellow and red. Sometimes one may pass a whole island of spicy fragrance—tiny little pinks, or huge scarlet-and-white carnations.[10]

It is more difficult to know how the Aztecs themselves felt about the aesthetics of vegetables in their *chinampas*. Motecuhzoma II was proud of his pleasure gardens, especially the botanical garden at Huaxtepec in the modern state of Morelos. During the time of the first Motecuhzoma (reigned 1440–1469), a garden "from the time of the ancestors" was discovered in ruins at Huaxtepec.[11] Motecuhzoma I had the garden's irrigation system and fountains restored and commanded the Lord of Cuetlaxtla to supply roots of cacao, vanilla orchid, magnolia, and other plants. Skilled gardeners accompanied the valuable gifts to the new garden and transplanted them after making appropriate offerings to Xochipilli.[12] When Cortés saw the Huaxtepec gardens some fifty years later, he described them as the "finest, pleasantest, and largest that ever was seen. . . . For the distance of two shots from a crossbow there were arbors and refreshing gardens and an infinite number of different kinds of fruit trees, many herbs and sweet scented flowers. It certainly filled one with admiration to see the grandeur and exquisite beauty of this entire orchard."[13] Another garden that impressed the Spaniards was that of a minor lord in Ixtapalapan. Bernal Diáz del Castillo (c. 1492–1584), of Cortés's army, offered this description:

The garden and orchard are most admirable. I saw and walked about in them and could not satiate myself sufficiently looking at the many kinds of trees and enjoying the perfume of each. And there were walks bordered with the roses of this country and flowers and many fruit trees and flowering shrubs; also a pool of fresh water. There was another thing worth seeing, namely, that large canoes could enter into the flower garden from the lagoon through an entrance they had made of many kinds of stone covered with polished stucco and painted, which gave one much to think about. . . . Again I say that I do not believe that in the whole world there are other countries known to compare with this one.[14]

Motecuhzoma II, however, does not seem to have been as enamored of vegetable gardens. In a story, perhaps apocryphal, written well after Motecuhzoma II's death, Dr. Cervantes de Salazar noted:

In these flower gardens Montezuma did not allow any vegetables or fruit to be grown, saying that it was not kingly to cultivate plants for utility or profit in his pleasance. He said that vegetable gardens and orchards were for slaves or merchants. At the same time he owned such, but they were at a distance and he seldom visited them.[15]

It is true that the king and his lords did not directly cultivate the *chinampas*, though they certainly ate its produce and admired their flowers. Yet, cultivation of *chinampas* was firmly rooted in the Aztec mythos. In recounting the story of their migration into the Valley of Mexico, the Aztecs emphasized the importance of learning the secrets of *chinampas* cultivation. At first, *chinampas* were important because the recent arrivals had to pay tribute, including fresh vegetables, to the ruling lord of the valley. Over time, the Aztecs transformed themselves from dependents to the rulers of the valley. Many of the early Aztec wars of conquest were fought specifically to gain control of the *chinampas* of their neighbors and extracting tribute from them.[16] While *chinampas* were never the sole source of food, they were a highly prized resource and a unique source of beauty in the burgeoning Aztec empire.

NOTES

CHAPTER 1
Of Cabbages and Kings:
Quintinie and the Baroque Vegetable Garden

1. Christopher Thacker, *The History of Gardens* (Berkeley: University of California Press, 1992),147–148.

2. Ibid., 153.

3. Jean-Baptiste de la Quintinie, *The Compleat Gard'ner* (London and New York: Garland Publishing, 1982), 138.

4. Frédéric Abergel, Stéphanie de Courtois, and François Moulin, *Préparation à la visite du potager du roi* (Versailles: École nationale supérieure du paysage, 1999), 8.

5. Ibid., 4.

6. Quintinie, *Compleat Gard'ner*, 138.

7. Ibid., 33.

8. Ibid., 36.

9. Ibid., 33.

10. Ibid., 35.

CHAPTER 2
Gardens of the Soul: Ming Vegetable Gardens

1. Craig Clunas, *Fruitful Sites: Garden Culture in Ming Dynasty China* (Durham: Duke University Press, 1996), 173.

2. Liu Song's "Poems on Living in Poverty," "Poems on Garden Life," "Poems on Looking after the Melons and Vegetables in the East Garden," translated in John W. Dardess, "A Ming Landscape: Settlement, Land Use, Labor and Estheticism in T'ai-ho County, Kiangsi," *Harvard Journal of Asiatic Studies* 49, no. 2 (1989): 330–331. The epigraph to this chapter comes from ibid., 329.

3. Ibid., 305.

4. One *mu* equals approximately one-seventh of an acre. According to a Ming dynasty agricultural treatise, a vegetable garden of ten *mu* was considered sufficient to feed a single family. (Clunas, *Fruitful Sites*, 40.)

5. Dardess, "Ming Landscape," 319.

6. Clunas, *Fruitful Sites*, 52.

7. Ibid., 67.

8. Ibid., 94.

9. Ibid., 100.

10. Joanna Handlin Smith, "Gardens in Ch'i Piao-chia's Social World: Wealth and Values in Late-Ming Kiangnan," *Journal of Asian Studies* 51, no. 1 (1992): 59–60.

11. Clunas, *Fruitful Sites*, 80, 89.

12. Ibid., 77.

13. Ibid.

CHAPTER 3
Banishing the Vegetable Garden from the Landscape

1. Humphrey Repton, quoted in Mary Palmer Kelley Cooper, "The Early English Kitchen Garden," M.A. thesis, Louisiana State University, 1977, 66.

2. Alexander Pope, quoted in Penelope Hobhouse, *Penelope Hobhouse's Gardening through the Ages: An Illustrated History of Plants and Their Influence on Garden-Style from Ancient Egypt to the Present Day* (New York: Simon & Schuster, 1992), 192.

3. Alexander Pope, quoted in Christopher Thacker, *The History of Gardens* (Berkeley: University of California Press, 1992), 182.

4. Alexander Pope, quoted in Stephen Switzer, *Ichnographia Rustica, or, The Nobleman, Gentleman, and Gardener's Recreation* (New York: Garland Publishing, 1982), xxi.

5. John Dixon Hunt, ed., *A Particular Account of the Emperor of China's Gardens, near Pekin/Jean Denis Attiret; translated by Joseph Spence. Unconnected Thoughts on Gardening: A Description of the Leasowes /William Shenstone. An Essay on Design in Gardening /George Mason* (New York: Garland Press, 1982), 129.

6. Joseph Addison admired the new style of gardening, but cautioned that "it might, indeed, be of ill consequence to the public, as well as unprofitable to private persons, to alienate so much ground from pasturage and the plough" ("On the Pleasures of Imagination, Paper IV," *Spectator* 414 [25 June 1712]: 109); see also William A. Brogden, "The *Ferme Ornée* and Changing Attitudes to Agricultural Improvement," in *British and American Gardens in the Eighteenth Century*, ed. Robert P. Maccubbin and Peter Martin (Williamsburg: The Colonial Williamsburg Foundation, 1984).

7. Brogden, "*Ferme Ornée* and Changing Attitudes," 40.

8. Addison, "Pleasures of Imagination," 109.

9. Cooper, "Early English Kitchen Garden," 72.

10. Ibid., 76f.

11. Stephen Switzer, *The Practical Kitchen Gardiner* (London: Thomas Woodard, 1727).

12. William Mason, *The English Garden: A Poem in Four Books* (1783), quoted in Cooper, "Early English Kitchen Garden," 85.

13. R. A. Dodsley, *A Description of the Leasowes, the Seat of the Late William Shenstone, Esq.*, in Hunt, *A Particular Account*.

14. Quoted in R. C. Bald, "Sir William Chambers and the Chinese Garden," *Journal of the History of Ideas* 11, no. 3 (1950): 292.

15. Thacker, *History of Gardens*, 182; Cooper, "Early English Kitchen Garden," 82; April Susan Potter, "The Kitchen Garden: An Historical Analysis and Review," M.A. thesis, Cornell University, 1986, 68f.

16. Reverend Hansbury, *The Compleat Body of Gardening and Plantings* (1778), quoted in Cooper, "Early English Kitchen Garden," 86f.

17. Ibid., 87.

18. The epigraph for this section is quoted in Edwin Morris Betts, ed., *Thomas Jefferson's Garden Book* (Charlottesville: Thomas Jefferson Memorial Foundation, 1999), 461.

19. Ibid., 544.

20. Ibid., 70f.

21. Ibid., 105.

22. Ibid., 634f.

23. Ibid., 111–114.

24. Ibid., 112.

25. Ibid., 360.

26. Rudy J. Favretti, "Thomas Jefferson's *Ferme Ornée* at Monticello." *Proceedings of the American Antiquarian Society* 103, no. 1 (1993): 17–29.

27. William L. Beiswanger, "The Temple in the Garden: Thomas Jefferson's Vision of the Monticello Landscape." In *British and American Gardens in the Eighteenth Century*, ed. Robert P. Maccubbin and Peter Martin (Williamsburg: The Colonial Williamsburg Foundation, 1984), 176, 185.

28. Thomas Jefferson, "General Ideas for the Improvement of Monticello," c. 1804. Thomas Jefferson Papers, Massachusetts Historical Society.

29. Quoted in Brogden, "*Ferme Ornée* and Changing Attitudes," 43.

30. Quoted in Potter, "The Kitchen Garden," 69.

31. Quoted in Charles Lyte, *The Kitchen Garden* (Oxford: The Oxford Press, 1984), 41.

32. Andrew Jackson Downing, "Notes to Rural Improvers," *The Horticulturist* 3, no. 1 (1848): 9–10.

33. George Kidd, gardener with Robert Donaldson, Esq., Blithewood, Dutchess County, N.Y., Red-Hook, N.Y., "A Hint on Kitchen Gardens," *The Horticulturist*, 3, no. 10 (1849): 471–472.

34. Edward Kemp, *How to Lay out a Garden* (New York: Birkenhead Park, 1858), 44.

CHAPTER 4
A Vegetable Garden Conundrum: Chimneys

1. Frederick Law Olmsted Jr. to Gardiner Martin Lane, March 21, 1902, Containers B28–B29, Job Number 273, Records of the Olmsted Associates, Manuscripts Division, Library of Congress.

2. Frances Benjamin Johnston, "Gardens by the Sea," *Country Life in America* (August 1925): 66–68; Mary Northend, "A North Shore Garden at Manchester-by-the-Sea," *American Homes and Gardens* (November 1907): 419–421; Louise Shelton, *Beautiful Gardens in America* (New York: Charles Scribners and Sons, 1924).

3. Emma G. Lane, *Garden Book 1903*; *The Garden, Vol. IV*; *Record V*, The Chimneys Collection, Archives of American Gardens, Smithsonian Institution.

4. Newspaper clippings in *Garden Book 1903*.

5. Memorandum by E. C. Whiting, August 12, 1947, Containers B28–B29, Job Number 273, Records of the Olmsted Associates.

6. Katharine Lane Weems (as told to Edward Weeks), *The Odds Were Against Me* (New York: Vantage Press, Inc., 1985), 10, 153.

7. Gardiner Martin Lane to Olmsted Brothers, April 27, 1903, Containers B28–B29, Job Number 273, Records of the Olmsted Associates.

8. Memorandum by Frederick Law Olmsted Jr., October 28, 1911, Containers B28–B29, Job Number 273, Records of the Olmsted Associates.

9. Frederick Law Olmsted Jr. to Gardiner Martin Lane, February 18, 1907, Containers B28–B29, Job Number 273, Records of the Olmsted Associates.

CHAPTER 5
The Vegetable Still Life

1. Norman Bryson, *Looking at the Overlooked: Four Essays on Still Life Painting* (Cambridge: Harvard University Press, 1990), 64–69.

2. Quoted in Brandon B. Fortune, "A Delicate Balance: Raphaelle Peale's Still Life Paintings and the Ideal of Temperance," in Lillian Miller, ed., *The Peale Family: Creation of a Legacy 1770–1870* (New York: Abbeville Press, 1996), 138.

3. Quoted in William H. Gerdts, *Painters of the Humble*

Truth: Masterpieces of American Still Life 1801–1939 (Columbia and London: Philbrook Art Center, University of Missouri Press, 1981), 52.

4. Quoted in Fortune, "A Delicate Balance," 138.

5. Linda Crocker Simmons, "James Peale: Out of the Shadows," in Miller, *The Peale Family*, 203–219.

6. Quoted in Sybille Ebert-Schifferer, *Still Life: A History*, trans. Russell Stockman (New York: Harry N. Abrams, Inc., 1998), 294.

CHAPTER 6
Vegetable Garden Victorious

1. David M. Tucker, *Kitchen Gardening in America: A History* (Ames: Iowa State University Press, 1993), 121–122.

2. Charles Lathrop Pack, *The War Garden Victorious* (Philadelphia: J. B. Lippincott Company, 1919), 10.

3. F.O.B. is a shipping term that stands for "Free on Board," meaning the seller is required to transport without cost to the buyer.

4. Pack, *War Garden Victorious*, 29, 30.

5. J. Horace McFarland, "The October War Garden View," *The Flower Grower: The Home Gardener Magazine*, October 1942, 439; "The Value of Flowers in War Time," *The Garden Club of America Bulletin*, August 1944, 35–38; "Roses in Wartime," *The Flower Grower: The Home Gardener Magazine*, March 1942, 125–126; Mrs. Walker Brewster, "War Bulletin May 1917," *The Garden Club of America Bulletin*, May 1945, 7; James Bush-Brown, "Home Food Production," *The Flower Grower: The Home Gardener Magazine*, February 1942, 68–69; W. D. Whitcomb, "Garden Pest Control in the Emergency," *The Flower Grower: The Home Gardener Magazine*, March 1942, 148–149.

6. Clarence Moores Weed, "Garden and Orchard," *The House Beautiful*, January 1918, 108.

7. Leonidas Willing Ramsey, "Make Your War Garden Attractive," *The Garden Magazine*, January 1918, 200–201.

8. Ibid., 201.

9. Elizabeth Strang, "Flowers for the War Time Garden," *The Garden Magazine*, April 1918, 137–139.

10. Brent Elliott, *The Country House Garden from the Archives of Country Life: 1897–1939* (London: Mitchell Beazley, 1995), 8f, 39.

11. Pack, *War Garden Victorious*.

12. Pack, *War Garden Victorious*, Appendix, p. 1; Joachim Wolschke-Bulmahn, "From the War Garden to the Victory Garden: Political Aspects of Garden Culture in the United States during World War I," *Landscape Journal* 11, no. 1 (1992): 51–57.

13. Agnes Selkirk Clark, "The Small Place: A Study in Planning a Balanced Garden," *House and Garden*, January 1944, 32–33.

14. Tucker, *Kitchen Gardening in America*, 133–135.

15. Marion Thomas, "What Is Going on in the Clubs and Societies?" *The Flower Grower: The Home Gardener Magazine*, February 1942, 81–82.

16. Marion Thomas, "What Is Going on in the Clubs and Societies?" *The Flower Grower: The Home Gardener Magazine*, May 1942, 234.

17. "Garden Clubs in Wartime," *The Flower Grower: The Home Gardener Magazine*, February 1942, 82.

18. Aline Kate Fox, "President's Message," *Garden Club of America Bulletin*, March 1942, 3; "That V Sign," *House and Garden Magazine*, November 1943, 1; Richardson Wright, "Victory Garden Harvest Shows," *House and Garden*, August 1942, 32–33.

19. Advertisements in *Flower Grower Magazine*, March 1942.

20. Tucker, *Kitchen Gardening in America*, 136.

21. Paul Frese, "1943: A Forecast," *The Flower Grower: The Home Gardener Magazine*, January 1943, 8.

22. "Gardeners Who Arm with Food," *House and Garden Magazine*, November 1943, 60–62; "Garden for Victory," *House and Garden Magazine*, October 1942, 42–44; H. W. Hochbaum, "Let's Have More and Better Victory Gardens in 1943," *The Flower Grower: The Home Gardener Magazine*, December 1942, 20–21.

23. Tucker, *Kitchen Gardening in America*, 136.

24. S.A.V.E., "Veg.," *Garden Club of America Bulletin*, February 1943, 28–29; March 1943, 19–21; April 1943, 28–29; May 1943, 20–21.

25. S.A.V.E., May 1943, 20.

26. June Platt, "My Victory over the Victory Garden," *House and Garden Magazine*, January 1944, 28–29.

27. Ogden Nash, "My Victory Garden," *House and Garden Magazine*, November 1943, 63.

28. "Flower Seed Farms Are Converting to Vegetables," *The Flower Grower: The Home Gardener Magazine*, June 1943, 311.

29. Martha Pratt Haislip, "Snip-and-Sniff Borders," *The*

Flower Grower: The Home Gardener Magazine, May 1942, 244.

30. Jean-Marie Putnam and Lloyd C. Cosper, *Gardens for Victory* (New York: Harcourt, Brace and Company, 1943), 24–38.

31. "Have Your Garden and Eat it Too!" *House Beautiful*, March 1942, 62–63.

32. Putnam and Cosper, *Gardens for Victory*, 25; Mrs. Thomas G. Spencer, "A Little 'Fence Victory Garden' for Food, Flavor, Fragrance and Fun," *Garden Club of America Bulletin*, August 1943, 12–13; Mrs. Randolph Rausch, "Ornamental Vegetable Gardening," *Garden Club of America Bulletin*, May 1945, 25.

33. J. Horace McFarland, *Breeze Hill News*, March 1942, 3–12.

34. Ibid., November 1942, 4.

35. Ibid.

36. For simplicity's sake, I use the term "Japanese American" to refer to both first-generation immigrants from Japan (the *issei*), who were prohibited by law from applying for citizenship, and to their children (the *nisei*), who were citizens by birth.

37. John Tateishi, ed., *And Justice for All: An Oral History of the Japanese American Detention Camps* (Seattle: University of Washington Press, 1984), 87.

38. Robert M. Jiobu, "Ethnic Hegemony and the Japanese in California," *American Sociological Review* 53, no. 3 (June 1988), 359; Yoshiko Uchida, *Desert Exile: The Uprooting of a Japanese-American Family* (Seattle: University of Washington Press, 1982), 123; Tateishi, *And Justice for All*, 9, 51, 154, 189.

39. Jeffery F. Burton, Mary M. Farrell, Florence B. Lord, and Richard W. Lord, *Confinement and Ethnicity: An Overview of World War II Japanese American Relocation Sites*, National Park Service, Publications in Anthropology 74, rev. ed. (Tucson: Western Archaeological and Conservation Center, 2000).

40. "War Relocation Authority Photographs of Japanese-American Evacuation and Resettlement, 1942–1945," University of California, Berkeley, The Bancroft Library (http://www.oac.cdlib.org:80/dynaweb/ead/calher/jvac/).

41. Gwenn M. Jensen, "System Failure: Health-Care Deficiencies in the World War II Japanese American Detention Centers," *Bulletin of the History of Medicine* 73, no. 4 (1999): 602–628; Jeanne Wakatsuki Houston and James D. Houston, *Farewell to Manzanar* (New York: Bantam Books, 1995), 30; Tateishi, *And Justice for All*, 110; Uchida, *Desert Exile*, 77.

42. Miné Okubo, *Citizen 13660* (Seattle: University of Washington Press, 1946), 97.

43. Tateishi, *And Justice for All*, 12, 120.

44. Ibid., 76.

45. Houston and Houston, *Farewell to Manzanar*, 95.

46. Patricia Nelson Limerick, "Disorientation and Reorientation: The American Landscape Discovered from the West," *The Journal of American History* 79, no. 3 (1992): 1021–1049, 1043.

47. Okubo, *Citizen 13660*, 149.

48. Ibid., 192–193.

49. Houston and Houston, *Farewell to Manzanar*, 97–99; see also Tateishi, *And Justice for All*, 96; Uchida, *Desert Exile*, 93.

50. Tateishi, *And Justice for All*, 13f; Uchida, *Desert Exile*, 100.

CHAPTER 7
The Glorious Vegetable Garden

1. W. Andrew, "Vegetable Gardening Is 'In' Again," *The Prairie Garden*, 32 (February 1975): 86–88; Hugh Wieberg, "The Vegetable Garden—Try Something Different in '76," *New England Gardening Magazine* 3, no. 3 (1976): 8–10; James D. Dilbeck and James M. Stephens, "Saint Johns Vegetable Gardens: Searching for Excellence," *Proceedings of the Florida State Horticulture Society* 107 (1994): 374–376.

2. Rosalind Creasy, *The Complete Book of Edible Landscaping* (San Francisco: Sierra Club Books, 1982), 38.

3. Adrian Higgins, "Out of the Ordinary; Rosalind Creasy's Feasts from the Garden," *The Washington Post*, 1 April 1999, Home sec., p. 14; Judith Sims, "A Walk in the Garden with the Pioneer of Edible Landscape," *The Los Angeles Times*, 25 February 1989, p. T-18.

4. Sally Johnson, "Getting Down and Dirty in the Garden Is Big Business," *New York Times*, 28 September 1996, Business/Financial sec.

5. Nancy R. Gibbs, "Paradise Found: America Returns to the Garden," *Time*, June 20, 1988; "Power Gardening: An Earthy Hobby Has Been Transformed into a Status Game by Boomers with Plenty of Money to Mulch," *Time*, June 19, 1995.

6. Charles Elliot, "How the Vegetable Patch Got Its Shape," *Horticulture* 97, no. 2 (2000): 29–30; Joy Larkcom, "Jean le Carré," *The Garden: Journal of the Royal Horticultural Society* 126, no. 7 (2001): 547–551.

7. Clarrisa Start, "Container Gardening Is an Option When Space Is Limited," *St. Louis Post-Dispatch*, 9 March 2000, p. 5.

8. Rebecca Gray, "Redesigning the Kitchen Garden," *Garden Design* 15 (1996): 50–57.

9. Betsy Beckmann, "The 15 Minute Farmer," *Garden Design* 15 (1996): 93–5; Harriet Heyman, "The Comfort of Fences," *Garden Design* 16 (1997): 64–71.

10. Marty Meitus, "Eat Your Weird Vegetables!" *Denver Rocky Mountain News*, 29 October 1997; Georgeanne Brennan, "Turnip Family Makes Room for a Flashy Cousin," *New York Times*, 17 August 1997, Style sec.; Joan Lee Faust, "In the Garden: Making the Radish Patch More Exotic," *New York Times*, 18 April 1999, Westchester Weekly sec.

11. Gray, "Redesigning"; Elisabeth Ginsburg, "In the Garden: Some Lessons of Old from Williamsburg," *New York Times*, 9 July 2000, Westchester Weekly sec.; Mac Griswold, "Garden Notebook: George Washington Gardened Here," *New York Times*, 3 June 1999, House & Home, Style sec.

12. Warren Schultz, "Our Garden's First Steps," *Garden Design* 16 (1997): 58–63.

13. David Kaufmann, "French Class," *Garden Design* 18, no. 7 (1999): 24; Larkcom, "Jean le Carré," 547.

14. Page Dickey, "Growing a Kitchen," *Garden Design* 18, no. 4 (1999): 74–85; Michael Gertley and Jan Gertley, *The Art of the Kitchen Garden* (Newton, Conn.: Taunton Books, 1999); Tovah Martin, "Well-Dressed Vegetables," *Horticulture* 98, no. 6 (2001): 54–60.

15. Nancy Sterman, "Locate the New Vegetable Garden," *Organic Gardening* 48, no. 3 (2001): 28.

16. Dick Tracey, "A Garden That Looks Good Enough to Eat," *Christian Science Monitor* 93, no. 163 (2001): 19; Sarah Gray Miller, "High Style: Down to Earth," *Garden Design* 16 (1997): 62–71.

17. Karen Dardick, "Landscapes That Are Good Enough to Eat: Tony Kienitz Mixes up His Designs with Okra, Artichokes and Other Edible Plants," *Los Angeles Times*, 15 October 2001, E-2.

18. Dorreen Bronwyn, "Not Regimental: Ornamental," *Waikato Times* (New Zealand), 6 February 1998, 13.

CHAPTER 8
Feast or Fancy: The Ornamental Vegetable

1. Angus Barber, "Ornamental Vegetables," *Flora* 26 (1980): 25–27; Clare Garner, "Are You Supposed to Catch the Bouquet—or Make Soup with It?" *Independent on Sunday*, 10 November 1996, 9; Tom Cardy, "Saying It with Vegetables," *The Evening Post* (Wellington, New Zealand), 16 September 1998, 19.

2. "A Vegetable Year," *The House Beautiful*, May 1917, 372.

3. "The Second Summer of Our Gardens," *The House Beautiful*, March 1918, 211.

4. S.A.V.E., "Veg," *Garden Club of America Bulletin*, February 1943, 28–29.

5. Mrs. Hillyer Brown, "Potted Plants Rationed," *Garden Club of America Bulletin*, May 1942, 23.

6. Edwin Way Teale, "Victory Flowers," *The Flower Grower*, October 1942, 441.

7. Mrs. R. J. Duncomb, "Okra Is Decorative," The Flower Grower, May 1942, 228; Daniel J. Foley, *Vegetable Gardening in Color* (New York: The Macmillan Company, 1943), 114.

8. Jean-Marie Putnam and Lloyd C. Cosper, *Gardens for Victory* (New York: Harcourt, Brace and Company, 1943), 35f.

9. "Horticultural Letters," *Bulletin of the Garden Club of America*, March 1943, 41; Foley, *Vegetable Gardening in Color*, 73; J. Horace McFarland, *Breeze Hill News*, November 1942, 3.

10. Putnam and Cosper, *Gardens for Victory*, 29; Mrs. Thomas G. Spencer, "A Little 'Fence Victory Garden' for Food, Flavor, Fragrance and Fun," *Garden Club of America Bulletin*, August 1943, 12–13.

11. K. T. Achaya, *Indian Food: A Historical Companion* (Delhi: Oxford University Press, 1994), 92.

12. Hui-Lin Li, "The Vegetables of Ancient China," *Economic Botany* 23, no. 3 (1969): 256.

13. Joan R. Piggott, "*Mokkan*: Wooden Documents from the Nara Period," *Monumenta Nipponica* 45, no. 4 (1990): 453–456.

14. Anne Walthall, "Village Networks, Sodai and the Sale of Edo Nightsoil," *Monumenta Nipponica* 43, no. 3 (1988): 295; David Pollack, "*Kyoshi*: Japanese 'Wild Poetry,'" *Journal of Asian Studies* 38, no. 3 (1979): 515.

15. Andrew M. Watson, *Agricultural Innovation in the Early Islamic World: The Diffusion of Crops and Farming Techniques, 700–1100* (Cambridge: Cambridge University Press, 1983), 70–71.

16. John Gerard, *The Herbal or General History of Plants: The Complete 1633 Edition as Revised and Enlarged by Thomas Johnson* (New York: Dover Publications, 1975), 344–345.

17. H. Carrington, "Two Unpublished Letters of Thomas Jefferson," *William and Mary Quarterly Historical Magazine* 17, no. 1 (1908): 19.

18. Henry Phillips, *History of Cultivated Vegetables: Comprising Their Botanical, Medicinal, Edible, and Chemical Qualities; Natural History; and Relation to Art, Science, and Commerce*, 2d ed. (London: H. Colburn and Co., 1822), 179–181.

19. As late as 1928, Marion Cran lamented that she could find no one to eat the eggplants that she grew in her English garden. Marion Cran, *The Joy of the Ground* (London: Herbert Jenkins, 1928), 135.

20. Andrew F. Smith, *The Tomato in America: Early History, Culture, and Cookery* (Columbia: University of South Carolina Press, 1994), 16.

21. Quoted in George Allen McCue, "The History of the Use of the Tomato: An Annotated Bibliography," *Annals of the Missouri Botanical Garden* 39 (1952): 319.

22. Quoted in McCue, "The History of the Use of the Tomato," 310.

23. Gerard, *The Herbal*, 346.

24. McCue, "The History of the Use of the Tomato," 305, 307–309.

25. Rebecca Rupp, *Blue Corn and Square Tomatoes: Unusual Facts about Common Vegetables* (Pownal, Vt: Storey Communications, 1987), 16.

26. Smith, *The Tomato in America*, 34.

27. Ibid., 32.

28. Ibid., 39.

29. Ibid., 42.

30. Jean Andrews, *Peppers: The Domesticated Capsicums* (Austin: University of Texas Press, 1995), 57.

31. Ibid., 11.

32. Ibid., 13–15.

33. Dave Dewitt and Paul W. Bosland, *Peppers of the World: An Identification Guide* (Berkeley: Ten Speed Press, 1996), 27–30.

34. Ibid., 23–34, 44.

35. Ibid., 57–61.

36. Adrienne Cook, "Peppers That Pack Some Heat," *Washington Post*, 14 June 2001, H-10; Thomas Christopher, "Bird Pepper," *Horticulture* 70, no. 7 (1992): 80; Dewitt and Bosland, *Peppers of the World*, 197.

37. Dewitt and Bosland, *Peppers of the World*, 95–96.

38. K. W. Littger and W. Dressendörfer, *The Garden at Eichstatt: The Book of Plants by Basilius Besler* (Cologne: Taschen Books, 2000), pls. 324–331, and notes.

39. E. Lewis Sturtevant, *Sturtevant's Notes on Edible Plants, Report of the New York Agricultural Experiment Station for the Year 1919*, ed. U. P. Hedrick (Albany: J. B. Lyon Company, 1919), 545f.

40. "Pass the Pepper," *Scientific American* 14, no. 13 (1858): 99; A. H. Curtiss, "A Visit to the Shell Islands of Florida," *Botanical Gazette* 4, no. 2 (1948): 118.

41. Andrews, *Peppers*, 6.

42. H. C. Irish, "A Revision of the Genus *Capsicum* with Especial Reference to Garden Varieties," *Missouri Botanical Garden Annual Report* (1898): 60.

43. *Garden and Forest Magazine* 2 (1889): 60; Hezekia Butterworth, "An Old-Fashioned Thanksgiving," *The Century Illustrated Monthly Magazine*, New Series 23 (1892): 40.

44. George Bria, "New Garden Varieties for the New Year," *Associated Press Wire*, 31 October 2001.

45. U. Körber-Grohne, *Nutzpflanzen in deutschland: Kulturegeschichte and Biologie* (Stuttgart: Konrad Theiss Verlag, 1984), 185.

46. Toby Hodgkin, "Cabbages, Kales, etc.," in *Evolution of Crop Plants*, 2d ed., ed. J. Smartt and N. W. Simmonds (London: Longman Scientific and Technical, 1995), 77.

47. Pliny, *Natural History, Volume 6 (Libri XX–XXIII)*, Loeb Classical Library (1989) 392, Book XX, Chapters xxxiv, xxxvi; Collette Gouvien and Marielle Hucliez, *Le Roman du Potager* (Rodex: Editions du Rouergue, 1994), 16; Phillips, *History of Cultivated Vegetables*, 98 (see n.18).

48. Hodgkin, "Cabbages, Kales," 79.

49. John Laurence, *Gardening Improv'd* (London: W. Taylor, 1718), 28.

50. Quoted in Susan Campbell, "Digging, Sowing and Cropping in the Open Ground, 1600–1900," in *The Country House Kitchen Garden 1600–1950*, ed. C. Anne Wilson (London: Sutton Publishing, 1998), 16–17.

51. Weeks, Edwin (Lord), "From Ispahan to Kurrachee,"

Harper's New Monthly Magazine 88, no. 524 (1894): 241.

52. Sturtevant, *Notes on Edible Plants*, 108.

53. J. C. R. Seager, Y. Sakanishi, and H. Fukuzumi, "Ornamental Kale Could Have a Future in Ireland," *Farm and Food Research* 4, no. 6 (1973): 124–125; H. Takeda, *Systematic List of Economic Plants in Japan* (Tokyo: General Headquarters, Supreme Commander for the Allied Powers, Natural Resources Section, 1949), 320.

54. Joachim Richter, "Zierkohl für das Blumenbeet," *Garten Praxis* 5 (1977): 246.

55. Patricia O' Gorman notes, in *Patios and Gardens of Mexico* (New York: Architectural Book Publishing, Co., 1979), that ornamental cabbages were planted in a formal garden in Mexico; see also Richter, "Zierkohl," 247; and Seager et al., "Ornamental Kale," 124.

56. George W. Johnson, *A History of English Gardening, Chronological, Biographical, Literary, and Critical: Tracing the Progress of the Art in This Country from the Invasion of the Romans to the Present Time* (1829); reprint, vol. 27, *The English Landscape Garden*, ed. John Dixon Hunt (New York: Garland Publishing, Inc., 1982), 363.

57. Linda Kulman, "The Ornamental Cabbage Patch," *U.S. News & World Report*, 123, no. 22 (1997): 14; Madeleine Gray, "A Kale and Hearty Veggie," *Toronto Star*, 29 November 2000.

58. D. E. Yen, *The Sweet Potato and Oceania: An Essay in Ethnobotany*, Bernice P. Bishop Museum Bulletin 236 (Honolulu: Bishop Museum Press, 1974), 22–23.

59. Ibid., 33.

60. Ibid., 34.

61. Redcliffe Salaman, *The History and Social Influence of the Potato* (Cambridge: Cambridge University Press, 1949), 71.

62. Ping-ti Ho, "The Introduction of American Food Plants into China," *American Anthropologist* 57 (1955), 193.

63. Yen, *The Sweet Potato and Oceania*, 81.

64. Salaman, *History and Social Influence of the Potato*, 425.

65. Ibid., 436.

66. Yen, *The Sweet Potato and Oceania*, 231.

67. Gerard, *The Herbal*, 487.

68. Salaman, *History and Social Influence of the Potato*, 444.

69. Ibid., 105.

70. Allan M. Armitage and James M. Garner, "*Ipomoea batatas* 'Margarita,'" *Hortscience* 36, no. 1 (2001): 178.

71. Daniel W. Gade, "Achira, the Edible Canna: Its Cultivation and Use in the Peruvian Andes," *Economic Botany* 20, no. 4 (1966): 407–415.

72. Achaya, *Indian Food*, 94.

73. Reimar von Schaafhausen, "*Dolichos lablab* or Hyacinth Bean: Its Uses for Feed, Food and Soil Improvement," *Economic Botany* 17, no. 2 (1963): 146–153.

74. R. K. Arora, "Job's Tears (*Coix lacryma-jobi*): A Minor Food and Fodder Crop of Northeastern India," *Economic Botany* 31 (1977), 358–366; Hui-Lin Li, "The Origin of Cultivated Plants in Southeast Asia," *Economic Botany* 24, no. 1 (1970), 12.

75. Harold F. Winters, "Ceylon Spinach (*Basella rubra*)," *Economic Botany* 17, no. 3 (1963): 195–199.

76. F. W. Martin, "A Second Edible Okra Species, and Its Hybrids with Common Okra," *Annals of Botany* 50, no. 2 (1982): 277–283.

77. Hui-Lin Li, "The Vegetables of Ancient China," *Economic Botany* 23, no. 3 (1969): 258.

78. Ibid., 256f.

79. Robert W. Pemberton, "Waterbloometjie (*Aponogeton distachyos*, Aponogetonaceae), a Recently Domesticated Aquatic Food Crop in Cape South Africa with Unusual Origins," *Economic Botany* 54, no. 2 (2000): 144–149.

80. Dilys Davies, *Alliums: The Ornamental Onions* (Portland: Timber Press, 1992), 12–26.

81. Sturtevant, *Notes on Edible Plants*, 92.

82. T. J. Riggs, "Carrot," in *Evolution of Crop Plants*, 2d ed., ed. J. Smartt and N. W. Simmonds (London: Longman Scientific and Technical, 1995), 478.

83. Rupp, *Blue Corn and Square Tomatoes*, 115f.

84. Brian L. Benson, Robert J. Mullen, and Bill B. Dean, "Three New Green Asparagus Cultivars: Apollo, Atlas and Grande and One Purple Cultivar, Purple Passion," *Proceedings of the VIII International Symposium on Asparagus*, eds. M. Nichols and D. Swain, ISHS Acta Horticulturae, vol. 415 (1996), 60.

EPILOGUE

An Aztec Garden of Ornamental Vegetables

1. Richard F. Townsend, *The Aztecs* (London: Thames & Hudson, 2000), 21–22.

2. Pedro Armillas, "Gardens on Swamps," *Science* 174, no. 4010 (1971): 657.

3. Ibid., 653.

4. Zelia Nuttall, "The Gardens of Ancient Mexico," in *Smithsonian Institution Annual Report for the Year Ending June 30, 1923* (Washington, D.C.: U.S. Government Printing Office, 1925), 453–464.

5. William M. Denevan, "Aboriginal Drained-Field Cultivation in the Americas," *Science* 169, no. 3946 (1970): 647–654; Edward E. Calnek, "Settlement Pattern and *Chinampa* Agriculture at Tenochtitlán," *American Antiquity* 37, no. 1 (1972): 104–115.

6. Cora M. O' Neal, *Gardens and Homes of Mexico* (Dallas: Banks Upshaw and Company, 1945), 195.

7. Nuttall, "Gardens of Ancient Mexico," 453.

8. Townsend, *The Aztecs*, 220.

9. Ibid., 119.

10. Cecile Hulse Matschat, *Mexican Plants for American Gardens* (Boston: Houghton Mifflin, 1935), 31f.

11. Nuttall, "Gardens of Ancient Mexico," 457; Townsend, *The Aztecs*, 179.

12. Nuttall, "Gardens of Ancient Mexico," 456; Townsend, *The Aztecs*, 178.

13. Nuttall, "Gardens of Ancient Mexico," 457.

14. Ibid., 454.

15. Ibid.

16. Townsend, *The Aztecs*, 71.

SELECTED BIBLIOGRAPHY

Note on Methodology

This project grew out of my dissertation research on the cultural history of vegetable gardens from prehistory to the modern day. As with all such research, it resulted from a perceived deficit in the field. Except for a few histories of kitchen gardening in America and Europe and some studies in the developmental anthropological literature, vegetable gardens have received short shrift from historians and scientists. The stories of individual vegetables are a little better known, but there is no well-defined, coherent secondary literature on vegetable gardens in the academy. My research was possible only because of the ongoing digitization of journals and books, past and present, which allow for full text or indexed searching. In a relatively short amount of time, I amassed articles, blurbs, and passing asides on vegetable gardens, numbering now in the hundreds. For all intents and purposes, my data has been generated by search engines, and then fleshed out by complementary research from these randomized starting points. By necessity, this methodology has led to a spotty treatment of the material, as I sought broad patterns in the cross-cultural history of vegetable gardens. However, without the ability to search thousands of articles, I doubt I would have stumbled upon Ming vegetable gardens, Japanese *mokkan*, pilfered ornamental cabbage in New Zealand or all the nineteenth-century asides buried in small paragraphs at the bottom of pages. The notes contain references to all these obscure treasures, but for those who would simply like to read more about vegetable gardens, the following are more readily available sources.

Abergel, Frédéric, Stéphanie de Courtois, and François Moulin. *Préparation à la visite du potager du roi*. Versailles: École nationale supérieure du paysage, 1999.

Achaya, K. T. *Indian Food: A Historical Companion*. Delhi: Oxford University Press, 1994.

Allen, Oliver E. *Gardening with the New Small Plants: The Complete Guide to Growing Dwarf and Miniature Shrubs, Flowers, Trees, and Vegetables*. Boston: Houghton Mifflin, 1987.

Andrews, Jean. *Peppers: The Domesticated Capsicums*. Austin: University of Texas Press, 1995.

Anthony, Diana. *The Ornamental Vegetable Garden*. Toronto: Warwick Publishing, 1994.

Betts, Edwin Morris, ed. *Thomas Jefferson's Garden Book*. Charlottesville: Thomas Jefferson Memorial Foundation, 1999.

Boswell, Victor R. "Our Vegetable Travelers." *National Geographic Magazine* 96, no. 2 (1949): 98–170.

Bryan, John E., and Coralie Castle. *The Edible Ornamental Garden*. San Francisco: 101 Productions, 1974.

Bryson, Norman. *Looking at the Overlooked: Four Essays on Still Life Painting*. Cambridge: Harvard University Press, 1990.

Burton, Jeffery F., Mary M. Farrell, Florence B. Lord, and Richard W. Lord. *Confinement and Ethnicity: An Overview of World War II Japanese American Relocation Sites*. National Park Service Publications in Anthropology 74 (1999/rev. 2000).

Campbell, Susan. "Digging, Sowing and Cropping in the Open Ground, 1600–1900." In *The Country House Kitchen Garden 1600–1950*. Edited by C. Anne Wilson, 9–35. London: Sutton Publishing, 1998.

Clarke, Ethene. *The Art of the Kitchen Garden*. New York: Alfred A. Knopf, 1987.

Clunas, Craig. *Fruitful Sites: Garden Culture in Ming Dynasty China*. Durham: Duke University Press, 1996.

Creasy, Rosalind. *The Complete Book of Edible Landscaping*. San Francisco: Sierra Club Books, 1982.

———. *The Edible Heirloom Garden*. Boston: Periplus Editions, 1999.

DeWitt, Dave, and Paul W. Bosland. *Peppers of the World: An Identification Guide*. Berkeley: Ten Speed Press, 1996.

Dorra, Mary T. *Beautiful American Vegetable Gardens*. New York: Clarkson Potter, 1997.

Dun-zhen, Liu. *Chinese Classical Gardens of Suzhou*. Translated by Chen Lixian. New York: McGraw-Hill, 1993.

Ebert-Schifferer, Sybille. *Still Life: A History*. Translated by Russell Stockman. New York: Harry N. Abrams, Inc., 1998.

Fortune, Brandon B. "A Delicate Balance: Raphaelle Peale's Still life Paintings and the Ideal of Temperance." In *The Peale Family: Creation of a Legacy 1770–1870*, edited by Lillian Miller, 135–149. New York: Abeville Press, 1996.

Gerard, John. *The Herbal or General History of Plants: The Complete 1633 Edition as Revised and Enlarged by Thomas Johnson*. New York, Dover Publications, 1975.

Gerdts, William H. *Painters of the Humble Truth: Masterpieces of American Still Life 1801–1939*. Columbia and London:

Philbrook Art Center; University of Missouri Press, 1981.

Gertley, Michael, and Jan Gertley. *The Art of the Kitchen Garden*. Newton, Conn.: Taunton Books, 1999.

Gessert, Kate. *The Beautiful Food Garden: Creative Landscaping with Vegetables, Herbs, Fruits and Flowers*. Pownal, Vt.: Storey Communications, 1987.

Gilmore, G., and H. Gilmore. *Growing Midget Vegetables at Home*. New York: Lancer Books, 1973.

Gouvien, Collette, and Marielle Hucliez. *Le roman du potager*. Rodex: Editions du Rouergue, 1994.

Hagy, Fred. *The Practical Garden of Eden: Beautiful Landscaping with Fruits and Vegetables*. Woodstock, N.Y.: The Overlook Press, 1990.

Hamilton, Geoff. *The Ornamental Kitchen Garden*. London: BBC Books, 1995.

Hobhouse, Penelope. *Penelope Hobhouse's Gardening through the Ages: An Illustrated History of Plants and Their Influence on Garden-Style from Ancient Egypt to the Present Day*. New York: Simon & Schuster, 1992.

Hoog, Simone. *The Way to Present the Gardens of Versailles by Louis XIV*. Translated by John F. Stewart. Paris: Editions de la Réunion des musées nationaux, 1992.

Houston, Jeanne Wakatsuki, and James D. Houston. *Farewell to Manzanar*. New York: Bantam Books, 1995.

Hunt, John Dixon, ed. *A Particular Account of the Emperor of China's Gardens, near Peking/Jean Denis Attiret (translated by Joseph Spence); Unconnected Thoughts on Gardening: A Description of the Leasowes/William Shenstone; An Essay on Design in Gardening/George Mason*. New York: Garland Press, 1982.

Inn, Henry. *Chinese Houses and Gardens*. Edited by Shao Chang Lee. New York: Bonanza Books, 1950.

Johnston, R. Stewart. *Scholar Gardens of China*. Cambridge: Cambridge University Press, 1991.

Körber-Grohne, U. *Nutzpflanzen in Deutschland: Kulturegeschichte und Biologie*. Stuttgart: Konrad Theiss Verlag, 1984.

Kramer, Jack. *Earthly Delights: Tubs of Tomatoes and Buckets of Beans*. Golden, Col.: Fulcrum Publishing, 1997.

Lablaude, Pierre-André. *The Gardens of Versailles*. London: Zwemmer, 1995.

Larkcom, Joy. *Creative Vegetable Gardening: Accenting Your Vegetables with Flowers*. New York: Abbeville Press, 1999.

Li, Hui-Lin. *The Garden Flowers of China*. New York: The Ronald Press Company, 1959.

Littger, K.W., and W. Dressendörfer. *The Garden at Eichstätt: The Book of Plants by Basilius Besler*. Cologne: Taschen Books, 2000.

Livingston, A.W. *Livingston and the Tomato with a Foreword and Appendix by Andrew F. Smith*. Columbus: Ohio State University Press, 1998.

Lyte, Charles. *The Kitchen Garden*. Oxford: The Oxford Press, 1984.

Maccubbin, Robert P., and Peter Martin, eds. *British and American Gardens in the Eighteenth Century*. Williamsburg: The Colonial Williamsburg Foundation, 1984.

Miller, Lillian, ed. *The Peale Family: Creation of a Legacy 1770–1870*. New York: Abbeville Press, 1996.

Okubo, Miné. *Citizen 13660*. Seattle: University of Washington Press, 1946.

Pack, Charles Lathrop. *The War Garden Victorious*. Philadelphia: J. B. Lippincott Company, 1919.

Phillips, Henry. *History of Cultivated Vegetables; Comprising Their Botanical, Medicinal, Edible, and Chemical Qualities; Natural History; and Relation to Art, Science, and Commerce*, 2d ed. London: H. Colburn and Co., 1822.

Putnam, Jean-Marie, and Lloyd C. Cosper. *Gardens for Victory*. New York: Harcourt, Brace and Company, 1942.

Quintinie, Jean-Baptiste de la. *The Compleat Gard'ner*. London and New York: Garland Publishing, 1982.

Roberts, Annie Lise. *Cornucopia: The Lore of Fruits and Vegetables*. New York: Knickerbocker Press, 1998.

Rupp, Rebecca. *Blue Corn and Square Tomatoes: Unusual Facts about Common Vegetables*. Pownal, Vt.: Storey Communications, 1987.

Salaman, Redcliffe. *The History and Social Influence of the Potato*. Cambridge: Cambridge University Press, 1949.

Smith, Andrew F. *The Tomato in America: Early History, Culture, and Cookery*. Columbia: University of South Carolina Press, 1994.

Sokolov, Raymond. *Why We Eat What We Eat: How the Encounters between the New World and the Old Changed the Way Everyone on the Planet Eats*. New York: Summit Books, 1991.

Sturtevant, E. Lewis. "Sturtevant's Notes on Edible Plants."
  Edited by U. P. Hedrick. *Report of the New York
  Agricultural Experiment Station for the Year 1919*.
  Albany: J. B. Lyon Company, 1919.

Switzer, Stephen. *Ichnographia Rustica, or, The Nobleman,
  Gentleman, and Gardener's Recreation*. New York:
  Garland Publishing, 1982.

Tateishi, John, ed. *And Justice for All: An Oral History of the
  Japanese American Detention Camps*. Seattle: University
  of Washington Press, 1984.

Thacker, Christopher. *The History of Gardens*. Berkeley:
  University of California Press, 1992.

Townsend, Richard F. *The Aztecs*. London: Thames & Hudson,
  2000.

Tucker, David M. *Kitchen Gardening in America: A History*.
  Ames: Iowa State University Press, 1993.

Uchida, Yoshiko. *Desert Exile: The Uprooting of a Japanese-
  American Family*. Seattle: University of Washington
  Press, 1982.

"War Relocation Authority Photographs of Japanese-American
  Evacuation and Resettlement, 1942–1945." University of
  California, Berkeley, The Bancroft Library On-Line
  Archive (http://www.oac.cdlib.org:80/dynaweb/ead/cal-
  her/jvac/).

Watson, Andrew M. *Agricultural Innovation in the Early
  Islamic World: The Diffusion of Crops and Farming
  Techniques, 700–1100*. Cambridge: Cambridge University
  Press, 1983.

Wilson, C. Anne, ed. *The Country House Kitchen Garden
  1600–1950*. London: Sutton Publishing, 1998.

Yen, D. E. "The Sweet Potato and Oceania: An Essay in
  Ethnobotany." *Bernice P. Bishop Museum Bulletin 236*.
  Honolulu: Bishop Museum Press, 1974.

Yun, Qian, ed. *Classical Chinese Gardens*. Hong Kong: Joint
  Publishing Company, 1982.

SMITHSONIAN INSTITUTION ACKNOWLEDGMENTS

Millions of visitors to the Smithsonian Institution in Washington, D.C., have wandered through its beautiful gardens and been impressed and inspired by the creativity of the seasonal plantings. What few visitors realize is that in addition to these ever-changing gardens created by our Horticulture Services Division, the Smithsonian houses the Archives of American Gardens—an astounding collection of nearly eighty thousand photographic images, including nearly three thousand hand-colored glass lantern slides from the 1920s and 1930s. It is our pleasure to collaborate with the Horticulture Services Division to share its collection with the nation through *American Garden Legacy* exhibitions. *Feast Your Eyes: The Unexpected Beauty of Vegetable Gardens* is the second exhibition in the series.

Curator and book author Susan J. Pennington has shaped *Feast Your Eyes* from the very beginning. Her interest in the cultural history of vegetable gardens, vast archaeological expertise, and special humorous flair have given the project unique style and flavor.

The exhibition has been organized and circulated by the Smithsonian Institution Traveling Exhibition Service (SITES) in cooperation with the Smithsonian's Horticulture Services Division (HSD). Our gratitude goes to HSD's Nancy Bechtol, director of the Office of Museum Support Services; Joyce Connolly and Paula Healy, museum specialists, for their guidance, support, and enthusiasm.

We extend thanks in equal measure to Fred Schaub for designing the exhibition. The Smithsonian's Office of Exhibits Central carried out the production of the exhibition under the guidance of Michael Headley, director; Mary Bird, assistant director; and Ann Carper, editor. We appreciate the assistance of Valerie Wheat, librarian, Smithsonian Institution Libraries, Horticulture Branch.

At SITES, we acknowledge the contributions of the project team for *Feast Your Eyes: The Unexpected Beauty of Vegetable Gardens:* Nona Martin, project director; Patsy-Ann Rasmussen, registrar; Frederica R. Adelman, directors of exhibits; Laurie M. Trippett and Fredric P. Williams, assistant director for exhibits; Sandra Narva, director of scheduling and exhibitor relations; and Michelle Torres-Carmona, senior scheduling and exhibitor relations coordinator.

This book's publication was directed by Andrea P. Stevens, director of external relations; it was edited by Ann C. Easterling, SITES.

As the exhibition begins its national tour, we extend our sincere appreciation to the institutions hosting *Feast Your Eyes: The Unexpected Beauty of Vegetable Gardens* for helping us share the exceptional collection of the Archives of American Gardens with their audiences.

Anna R. Cohn
Director, Smithsonian Institution
Traveling Exhibition Service

INDEX OF PLANT NAMES

Scotch Bonnet chili.
See Capsicum chinense Jacq.
Solanum melongena L., 97–100,
99. *See also* eggplant
sweetpotato, 13, 18, 25, 95, 121,
122. *See also Ipomoea batatas*
(L.) Lam
sweetpotato vine, 95, 97, 107,
110, 112–113

Swiss chard, 62, 65, 97. *See also*
Beta vulgaris L.
tabasco pepper. *See Capsicum*
frutescens L.
tomato, 25, 27, **48,** 49, 58, 60, 65,
67, 74, 96, 97, 121, 122.
See also love apple;
Lycopersicon esculentum Mill.

vine spinach. *See Basella alba* L.

water hawthorn
(*Waterbloometjie*).
See Aponogeton distachyos L.
wild flea pepper. *See Capsicum*
annuum var. aviculare [Dierb.]
D'Arcy & Eshbaugh

INDEX OF PROPER NAMES

FEAST YOUR EYES

Produced by Joseph N. Newland, Q.E.D.
Design and composition by Catherine Mills Design, Seattle
Manuscript edited by Patricia Kiyono
Editorial assistance by Shariann Michael
Proofread by Mary E. Ryan
Index by Ann C. Easterling

Printed by Friesens, Manitoba, Canada

Titling set in Engravers
Text set in Trump Mediaeval